M000239978

Bohemian Magick

To Helen,
WHO WATCHES
OVER ME.

To David,
WHO WALKS
BESIDE ME.

Bohemian Magick

Witchcraft & Secret Spells

TO ELECTRIFY YOUR LIFE

VERONICA VARLOW

HARPER DESIGN
An Imprint of HarperCollins Publishers

CONTENTS

YOUR LIFE IS THE GREATEST SPELL YOU WILL EVER CAST.

Let me tell you why.

YOU ALREADY POSSESS A UNIQUE magick. Whether you've forgotten it, abandoned it, buried it, have an inkling of it, or are in touch with it, this magickal book of Bohemia will help you unlock, welcome, and nurture your truest self. With each day that this book is in your possession, with each spell that you cast, each potion that you brew, and each invocation that you pronounce and send out to the universe, you will be reminded of your own raw power.

My fortune-telling Ancestors would say that the mark of fate crossing the lines of your palms brought you to this very moment, that holding this book of lost spells of Bohemia in your hands is destiny.

Y NAME IS VERONICA, THE LAST DAUGHTER in a long line of Bohemian Witches. The foundation of my family's magick reaches back five generations to the westernmost part of what was once Czechoslovakia, the mystical lands known to poets and lovers as Bohemia. My Ancestors hailed from this Old World of mystics and adventurers, a place of wooden wagons vividly painted with stars and crescent moons, their interior walls covered with lush velvet fabrics in a kaleidoscope of colors and hand-carved wooden shelves hosting clusters of dripping candles decorated with symbols. The supernatural treasures of these wagons might include a worn pack of playing cards or a crystal ball used to divine the future, and corked bottles containing potions, herbs, and oils awaiting their purpose in magick spells. A bonfire crackles in the night outside as the community of people from neighboring wagons come together to play guitars and tambourines, to sing in the night and tell stories that will be passed on for generations.

These are my people. Many of the stories and traditions passed on at that bonfire have been lost. But in the early 1900s, my great-grandmother Anna was there. A child, she hung onto every word. When the day came that she crossed the seas to America, she held onto the traditions of magick so she could whisper them in her future daughter's ear as her own mother had whispered them to her.

Anna's first-born daughter, Helen Rose, was born of a difficult labor during the Great Depression, arriving with what my family referred to as the "veil." A veiled, or "caul," birth is a rare phenomenon; it occurs when a thin layer of the amniotic sac is still attached to the baby's face and head when it is born. Bohemian folklore says that those born with the veil have the supernatural gift of second sight and may have the ability to see or speak to the Spirits. I can tell you that this Bohemian folklore is true.

Helen was my grandmother.

She was a woman of magick and spells, a whirl of peroxide-blonde curls and Lucky Strike cigarettes. She was a woman of black cat-eye sunglasses, painted ruby-red nails, and a wild cackling laugh that boomed through a room. She loved her candles and singing out loud with the silver transistor radio that crackled in her kitchen.

She has been dead for decades longer than she was alive during my life. Yet, the secret spells in this book, the threads of the things she taught me, summon her vibrant spirit. She cradles me through the curves of the spells that I draft in my grimoire.

My Czech-Romani grandmother Helen handed her magick down to me, as it had been handed down to her over five generations in Bohemia, from first daughter to first daughter.

On certain days, when I'm speaking a magickal incantation, my voice changes, and the sound that comes out of my mouth hums with the cadence of her own.

She is the inspiration for this book.

She is in this book.

She lives in my bones.

I am the FIRST DAUGHTER but I am also the LAST.

Anna & Helen Rose
(Age 5)

Grandma Helen

Nincy + Me ♡

Me as a BROWNIE SCOUT.

I HAVE A MEMORY OF A PIVOTAL MOMENT IN MY eighth year: getting off the school bus as fast as I could and running to Grandma Helen's house in tears after kids hurled insults at me, making fun of my buck teeth and the fact that I was so much taller than they were.

As I cried, my Grandma wrapped her arm around my shoulders and walked me down to the dock on the lagoon. She brushed my hair as we sat on the edge of the creaky wooden planks, the murky waters just a few inches away from the bottom of my sneakers. She was always fussing with my hair and telling me stories. I remember watching the shadows of my swinging legs reflected in the water of the lagoon. I remember wanting to dive in and disappear.

14

My Grandma continued pulling the brush through my hair as tears fell down my face. When she was done, she gathered the puffy cloud of my hair out of the brush and put it beside the dock under a small rock.

"Watch," she whispered.

The afternoon sun made the water sparkle brightly, as if diamonds were bouncing on the tide. We had been watching the strands of my hair under the rock for a long time when suddenly a little brown bird hopped down and took some of the hair in its beak. It flew away, and then returned, taking more. This happened several times, until all the hair was gone.

My Grandma turned to me and said, "Are you really worried about other people's opinions of you when you know now that baby birds will sing their first song nestled in your hair? You are magick, you have to know that. What other people think of you isn't any of your business."

Her words woke me up to the essence of life:

> When you stop worrying about what
> other people think of you,
> you make room for your own magick
> to thrive.

Every spring since then, no matter where I am in the world, I have performed this ritual: the brushing, the placing of hair under a small rock, the waiting, and then, inevitably, *she* arrives. The mother bird flies in and lands. Wordlessly, I watch her, as she flies back and forth until the strands that I leave are gone.

I stand alone, remembering the girl I once was, who sat on the dock with her grandmother. Generations of mother birds have carried back my hair in their beaks to make their homes. Generations of baby birds have opened their tiny mouths to sing their first song in nests woven with a part of me.

The baby birds will have a home in the strands of my hair until the end of my days. Golden feathers and raven feathers decorate my hair now. They have a story of their own, an unspoken pact, a remembrance of my grandmother and of the birds who gave me my first glimpse of the Wild.

The Wild is my name for the purest, most ancient magick within you.

When we were very small children, we were the closest to our Wild that we will ever be; after all, we didn't know how to be anything but our truest selves. Early childhood was a time when we could access our own unique magick more easily. The world hadn't yet taught us to conceal who we are to fit in. The world hadn't taught us to hide our Wild yet.

The Wild is a powerful life-force energy within us that carries instinctive knowledge spanning from the beginning of time. It is a knowing. It is the supernatural force of your instinct and intuition that can guide you like an internal compass.

The Wild lives in the strength in your being that rises up when you allow your genuine self to thrive. It is the courage to do things your way, to use your voice and your truth to stand up for yourself, for those who cannot, and for this earth, and to walk through this world like you've got an army of summoned Spirits at your side. The Wild lives in your own secret understanding to speak the language of the forest, the wind, the fire, and the river. It is in the deep magick of embracing the electric essence of your life-force energy.

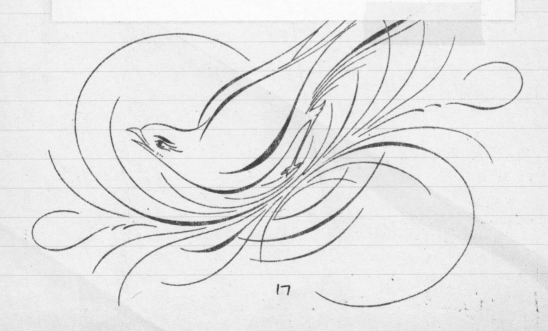

Grandma Helen embraced the Wild, even if she didn't call it that, because she trained me in the ways of magick from the time I was six years old, just as her mother had trained her. Grandma Helen was gifted in all the ways of divination and Spirit speaking. She would teach me rhyming incantations for spells as she pushed me on the swing in the backyard. I spent weekends at her house, carving magick candles with my Brownie pocketknife under her close watch. She would pull out her blue tarot deck covered in stars and tell me the stories of every card. I memorized the significance of the colorful pictures like I was learning another language.

She also taught me how to talk to our friends, the Spirits. She told me they were Ancestors of our family, friends, and animals that had crossed over to the Otherside and looked after us. She showed me how to light a candle to call to these Spirits "just like a lighthouse in the night."

She taught me to see the future by closing my eyes and imagining myself walking into an underground cave, a safe place with a burning bonfire at its center and drawings and symbols written on the walls. Once I could see the space itself clearly, she would ask what I saw on the walls. Pictures formed in my mind, and more often than not, what I described seeing on the walls would happen. Little predictions that came true, like knowing that my Great-Aunt Irene was going to call and tell us she had bought an antique spinning wheel like the one from *Sleeping Beauty* or that my Grandma's friend was going to show up wearing a yellow dress covered in daisies. These were small occurrences but things that I could not have known otherwise. They were there on the walls of the cave in my mind.

I would go to the safe cave in my mind and talk to the Spirits anytime I wanted to and about anything I wanted to. Grandma assured me that the Spirits loved me and wanted to help me. They were like family to us, she would say. My Grandma would blow smoke rings in the kitchen and pace the floor to talk to them, and I would copy her with my candy cigarettes, blowing the powdered sugar on the gum in the rolled-up white paper into the room like little ghosts. This wasn't particularly unusual in our home; my family embraced the supernatural. My Mom has prophetic dreams, my brother Rion reads palms, and my Dad sees the future in the flickering of candle flames.

My Mom & Dad

THE SUMMER I TURNED TWELVE, NOT LONG after Grandma Helen came home from the hospital after having heart surgery, we were sitting in her rock garden, carving candles in the afternoon sun. She explained that as our magick candles burn down, they start to form again on the Otherside for us. She said that when our candles disappear here on earth, they are fully formed and burning for us on the Otherside, as if they are keeping the light glowing for our magickal wishes to come true. "It will be easy for you to find me over there one day, Valentine Face," she said. "Just look for the City of Candles, and I'll be there."

A few months later, I woke up to the sound of the phone ringing in the middle of the night, then a short silence, then my Dad wailing. I didn't have to ask why. I remember sitting up in my bed with a sense of overwhelming loss.

I knew that Grandma had gone to her City of Candles.

Seven years later, I left the small Florida town where I grew up, my car packed with all my earthly possessions, and drove twenty-four hours north to my own city of lights, New York City. I found a sublet on Bleecker Street, a studio apartment with a shower room down the hall, a place where heroin addicts would shoot up and nod off on a regular basis. I worked two jobs—as a waitress two nights a week and as tour guide on a double-decker bus the rest of the time—to put myself through New York University. I quickly realized that my one hard priority was keeping a roof over my head. I had no time for spells and incantations. I had to *survive*. The crush of days almost obliterated my own magick entirely.

Then I met the Black Dog. On an unseasonably warm day at the end of December, I was finishing my shift as a volunteer at a Brooklyn animal shelter. I had taken a dozen dogs for solo walks that day and was about to leave, when I was asked to take another dog out, a large Rottweiler that had just been newly admitted to the shelter. The dog was casting her sad eyes toward me—I couldn't say no.

Five minutes later, we were walking the four blocks to the park under the Williamsburg Bridge. The dog sat down in a beam of sunshine on the gravel parking lot while I sat on the high concrete curb beside her.

I remember having a feeling of peace in those moments, just sitting there with her in the sun, watching the waves move on the East River in front of us. Suddenly, a utility truck in the parking lot backed into reverse, sounding a loud, high-pitched beeping alarm. I whipped my head around to make sure the driver saw us sitting there, and before I knew what happened, the terrified Rottweiler's front paws were on my shoulders. She knocked me from a sitting position to my back, flat out on the concrete, as she sunk her teeth into my face.

The next thing I knew, doctors leaned over me, weaving black threads to stitch a good portion of my nose back to my face as blurry nurses pressed gauze against my injured left eye to cover it. There were moments lying there amid the beeping machines, bright lights, and the smell of bleach when I felt I was hovering outside my body in a way that I can only guess would be akin to the seconds before we are born.

Operating rooms are places where birth and death are easy neighbors. They are places where the person lying on the table inevitably runs through the same series of questions that every person who has lain on that table has gone through.

It is the Reckoning.

In shock, I stared at the irregular texture of the acoustic-tile dropped ceiling above me, questions flooding my brain, questions we all ask ourselves when Death peeks in the room.

Why did this happen to me?

What was this life all about?

What is going to happen?

Why did I waste so much time?

Who have I been all these years?

Why had I not done the things that
I wanted to do?

There are many ways to explain away what happened that day or why things happened the way they did. But I know the real reason:

I had turned my back on my own magick.

I had lost touch with my Wild, my truest self. I was afraid to be her. In fact, being her felt like the most dangerous thing I could do. I had let my fears stop me from taking risks. I had done what Grandma Helen told me not to do: I had made what others thought about me my business. I was dying inside because I had denied my Wild.

I know you know what I mean. It's a numbness that creeps in when you're just going through the motions of getting through a day. It's losing the meaning of what your life is all about just to get a paycheck and have a place to sleep. When we tell our Wild to be quiet, our soul hears it too, and it starts to die slowly.

Before I met the Black Dog, I didn't take risks. I didn't follow my dreams. I turned my back on my magick; I didn't make time for it. All the bills and all the pressures of life made me forget who I truly was. Now I see the Black Dog as an angel who snapped me alive; on that day, I saw things for what they were and I have not looked back since. My wish is that this book can serve you in the same way.

May you not have to endure an experience this extreme to awaken your truest self, your Wild, Dear Witch. That's why I've told you this story: to help you call in your own power, your self-awareness, and your confidence—just as the ghost of the Black Dog does for me.

Resurrect your Wild, my Love. Live your life with the full force of your own naked eternal song, quivering with all that you have ever been and all that you are.

This world needs you to rise in your magick more than ever.

It can no longer be hidden away.

Whether you've claimed the word "Witch" out loud, or tried it on in a whisper under the glow of the moon, summon your strength to speak it now—we've got a legacy to live. Get out your broom. Tonight we ride!

Enchant This Book to You

HEN ENCHANTED BY A WITCH, INANIMATE objects are filled with a life-force energy. In the magick of Bohemia, tarot cards, wands, crystals, potion bottles, brooms, and grimoires take on a living personality when infused with the breath, intention, and energy of their magickal master. Before we begin, let's enchant this book to you, as it will be both your companion and guide to the world of Bohemian magick.

The first step in any spell is to know your intention. Your intention for performing this spell is to enchant this book to you as a mystical companion and lifelong friend who will journey with you into the magick of Bohemia. You will do this through using your unique magick force to bond with this book and enchant it with life as described in the steps taught to me by my Grandma Helen.

TOOLS AND MATERIALS

✦ Altar
✦ Pillow or soft blanket
✦ One seven-inch red taper candle
✦ Candleholder
✦ Lighter or matches
✦ Small hand mirror
✦ Your favorite lipstick
✦ A hairbrush
✦ Clear tape

CAST THE SPELL

1. Bearing your intention fully in mind, begin by setting your magickal tools before you on your altar—a shelf or small table that you have decided to dedicate to your magickal workings. Get comfortable and sit before your altar on a pillow or a soft blanket.

2. Set the candle in its holder in the center of your altar and light it. In the lore of Bohemia, lighting a candle signals the parting of the veil between the earthly plane and the realm of the Spirits. The candle flame is meant to call Ancestors and the Spirits to your workings with its light.

3. Take the hand mirror and hold it in your Spirit hand (nondominant hand). In the mirror illuminated by the candlelight, look into your eyes. Notice their color; focus deeply on them, almost as if you were hypnotizing yourself. Feel the power of your inner Witch coming to meet you.

4. With your dominant hand, slowly apply your lipstick. As you do this motion, imagine that you are enchanting your mouth to speak your truth.

5. Take your brush and brush your hair with nine strokes. Tape the strands of hair that have come out of the brush to this page. Your strands of hair contain your own powerful, unique code of DNA, and taping them to this book is the magickal equivalent to writing your name here and declaring this grimoire as your own.

MY HAIR

6. Once you've taped the strands of your hair to this page, hold this book against your heart and breathe deeply, nine times, in and out. Visualize golden beams of sunlight coming out of your heart and flooding onto the pages of this book. Imagine every page in the book glowing with power.

7. Press this book page to your lips and place your enchanted kiss print upon it. Just like in the faerie tale books, your kiss brings life and enchantment to this magickal grimoire.

MY LIPSTICK KISS

8. Now you will supernaturally charge this book with your own unique energy using the following Bohemian method: cup your hands in front of you as if you were going to drink water from a stream and close your eyes. Imagine yourself as a powerful Witch, strong, enchanted, and brave. Straighten your spine. Hold your head high. Imagine a bolt of iridescent lightning igniting raw power within you. When you can picture this clearly, blow into your cupped hands to write this new vision of yourself into the lines of your palms and give your spell life.

9. Close your hands, palm facing palm, flat, in a prayer position. Start to rub your hands back and forth quickly to cause friction and build energy around your vision. When it feels like your hands are burning hot with energy, quickly place your open palms onto these two pages of the book. Close your eyes and feel the power of your magickal force bonding with this book. This is how my Grandma Helen and the Bohemian people would charge magickal items.

10. Repeat this incantation three times, each time making your voice stronger and more forceful than the last:

```
      Book of Wisdom, sorcery, and spell
      Secrets of Bohemia which you shall
                  foretell.
      Potion, practice, charm, and brew,
    Provide me the sight and keep me true
        By fire, water, earth, and air,
        Enchanted by my strands of hair
   I charm this grimoire from page to spine
       It knows my name for it is mine.
        Sacred knowledge before my eyes,
          I summon my power and . . .
                Behold, I rise.
```

11. Take the candle from the center of your altar and pour some of the wax onto this page. Let wax cool slightly and then press your index finger into the wax so that your unique fingerprint appears there. Make sure you keep this book open for the next thirty minutes to let the fingerprint cool and set.

12. Blow out the candle and allow the smoke to drift to the sky so the Spirits and Ancestors receive your intention of this book being an enchanted companion of wisdom and magick for your journey. Finish by saying the magickal words that we use to cast a spell in the Witchcraft of Spectaculus:

```
   See it. Be it. So be it.
```

PART I

THE Spectaculus School OF Spellcasting

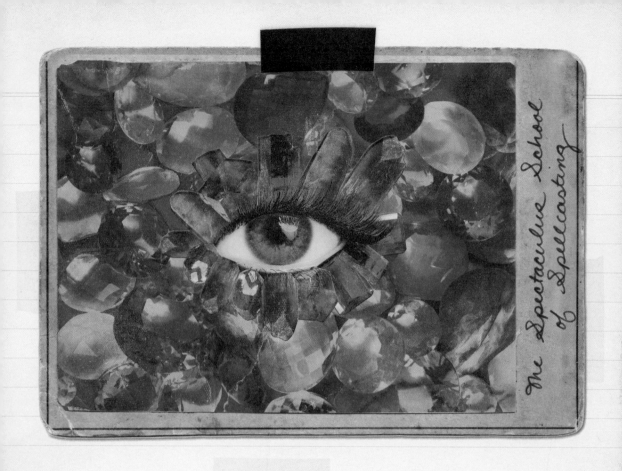

The Spectaculus School of Spellcasting

WELCOME TO THE WILD WITCHCRAFT OF Spectaculus, where every hour is the Witching hour and you are exactly where you belong—living your magickal Wild with all of us.

This book isn't presenting just any kind of basic Witchcraft, babe. This is Spectaculus—the deep, wild, naked, artistic supernova of Witchcraft. Spectaculus is an established branch of Witchcraft that I founded with my husband, David Garfinkel-Varlow. Spectaculus's roots are born in the Bohemian traditions of Grandma Helen and branch into our unique rock-and-roll magick that incorporates natural mysticism and instinctive creativity. All the secret traditions that you'll find in this book have been passed down through my Bohemian lineage or are spells, ceremonies, and magick techniques that I have invented.

31

This is the first time I have ever shared these secrets.

MY GRANDMA HELEN'S MAGICK WAS THE Witchcraft of the working class. She read tea leaves from a torn-open Lipton's bag and laid down well-worn playing cards to read the future after her chain-smoking, whiskey-drinking poker games with the ladies. Along with sharing my Grandma's magick, I'll show you the mystical ropes. My own brand of magickal spellcasting is a bit more adventurous, with a bent toward the sensual and the experimental. Spectaculus is the Witchcraft of the wanderers, the misfits, the artists, and the poets.

I tell you all this because there are many different traditions in Witchcraft. The Witchcraft of Spectaculus has carved its own mystical path guided by the old candle flame burning from Bohemia, the words of rock-and-roll troubadours, and the haunting and soulful sound of blues guitars.

Spectaculus is not about power over others. Spectaculus is about finding the power within yourself, no matter where you come from, no matter what your past is, no matter what's in your bank account. Spectaculus is anti-elitist, anti-establishment witchcraft. There are no levels that are higher in stature or better than others. We respect each other as equals. Spectaculus is the Witchcraft counterculture. It is a powerful melting pot of magick, with Witches of every skin color, background, shape, size, gender variant, and nonbinary. We recognize that there is a leader and a teacher in every single one of us, and we encourage sharing, adventuring, letting our imaginations run wild, and supporting each other in our journeys. We learn from each other's experiences and personal life stories. We are revolutionary magick workers who work spells and use our voices for equality, freedom, and opportunity for all people as we fight oppression. We know this to be true: we are strong as individuals and even more powerful when we stand together.

The SPECTACULUS CODE of HONOR

AS YOU DELVE INTO THE SECRETS contained in this grimoire, as you learn techniques from the Spectaculus School of Spellcasting and engage in the journeys and spells in the five initiations in Part II, it is important that you honor and pay respect to the origins of this magick when you practice it, both privately and publicly. By participating in this journey, you are now part of the legacy of Spectaculus and you are carrying on the high honor of keeping the work alive.

You have my permission to create any spell in this book and use the spells, techniques, and rituals in your own Covens as long as you acknowledge the Spectaculus tradition by name. Acknowledgment through word, through deed, and through writing honors the Craft and those who practiced it before you. Passing off these traditions as your own or not giving credit where it is due is bad mojo and will diminish your magickal workings. Always remember that when you cast your spells with honor, tradition, and dignity, the love will continue on and circle back to you.

Spellcasting the Spectaculus Way

SPELLS ARE WORDS WE SPEAK OR ACTIONS WE take to create or change energy.

Casting powerful spells is part of the primal power of being a Witch. It might seem intimidating at first, but the truth is you've been casting spells since you were old enough to make a wish and blow out candles on your birthday cake.

Mr. Mojo Risin`!
LOS ANGELES, July 1968

YES, YOU'VE BEEN CASTING SPELLS FOR THE majority of your existence, even if you weren't aware of it.

"I wish," "I am," "I desire," "I need"—these are the beginnings of tiny spells that wander easily from our lips in passing conversation all the time. They are unintentional spells.

In this section, I'm going to teach you how to craft powerful *intentional* spells. I will reveal my personal Spectaculus traditions that will help you rise exponentially in your own spellcasting power. I've crafted five potent steps to guide you to conjure spells with electrifying intention, spells that will jolt your wildest dreams into existence.

The Spectaculus way of casting spells is inherently powerful because the five steps are deeply personal, from giving yourself permission to summon all of your power to preparing your ritual space for the supernatural, adding pieces of your DNA and unique creative fire, and then by raising the energy to cast your spell with some of Grandma Helen's Bohemian magick!

The five steps of Spectaculus spellcasting are designed to electrify your magick, rocketing your spells into a whole new realm of Witchcraft. Remember, the amount of energy and thought you put into a spell is a good barometer of what you can expect in return.

I will show you how to connect to the powerful process of spellcasting and how to use your unique creativity to heighten your spell's potency. Plus, after I teach you the steps, I'll give you solid examples about how you can then write and cast your own original spells.

I highly recommend writing your spells in a dedicated journal. When you take time to write spellwork in your own hand, you not only validate your magick, but also create a record of it. This book of spells, magickal studies, and findings is what we Witches call a grimoire. You'll be thankful you created this most personal book: when you need to refer to a spell or any of your observations, your grimoire will hold them all, powerful reminders of your craft.

Crack open your grimoire, my dear Witch.

Spectaculus Spellcasting School
is now in session!

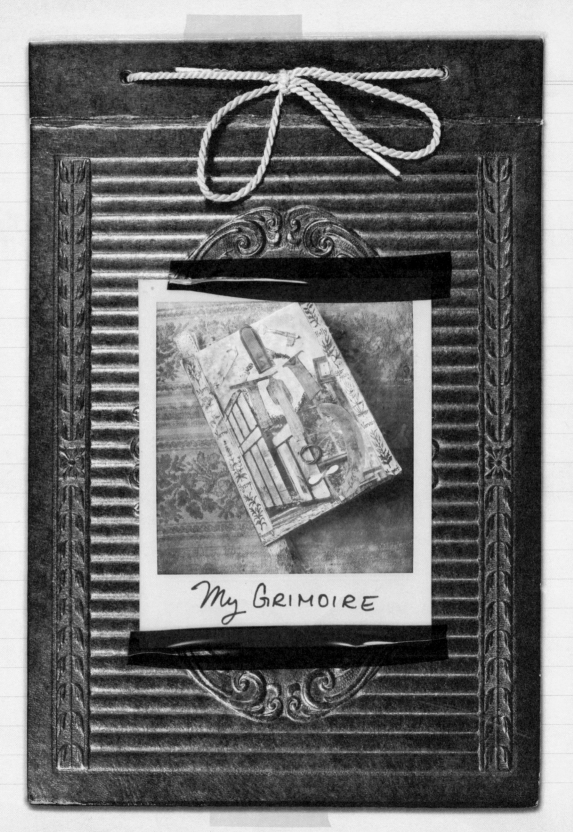

My Grimoire

STEP ONE
The Permission Slip

SPELLCASTING STARTS WITH YOUR PERSPECTIVE.

You are the boss of the spell.

Your words are your wands.

You must give yourself permission to own your magick.

To craft a hard-hitting spell, your mindset needs to be courageous, positive, and ready to weave the world to your desire. Let's face it, most times, when we are preparing to cast a spell, we're doing it because we feel a lack of something, like love, money, success, or confidence. How are we supposed to do a powerful confidence spell when our eyeliner is dripping down our face in black rivers?

You must call your power back to you.

Enter the Permission Slip.

The Permission Slip is the act of writing down your own strong statement, to give yourself permission to evoke the most powerful version of yourself. Free yourself and unleash your Wild! Ask yourself these questions and write down your answers:

> **What permissions should I grant myself in order to stand in my fullest power?**

Your answers should start with "I grant myself permission to . . ."

> **What bold statements am I willing to write and sign my name to that empower me fully?**

Your answers should be active. They should begin with "I," followed by a verb, such as "I create," "I speak," or "I weave."

Here is an example of what a Permission Slip might look like:

I grant myself permission to stand in my
** FULL POWER **
I grant myself permission to be vulnerable, raw, and
true to myself without shame.

I grant myself permission to invoke the wisdom
in my bones
from this lifetime
And from all others before it. *

I grant myself permission to tap into the legacy
of my ancestors
And the knowledge buried in my DNA,
both known and unknown to me.
• • •
I create with my word *
I speak spells into existence *
I weave my destiny
with all the love, power, and divinity
that courses through the blood in my veins.

* See it. Be it. So be it. *
*

Below my statement, I sign my name in bold and looping cursive as if I'm signing over a check to myself for one hundred million dollars. Own it. Your mindset is riches!

In your grimoire, write your Permission Slip. Create your own or use mine or make changes or additions as you see fit. When you are finished writing it, read it out loud at least three times, amplifying your voice with authority, until you feel the power vibrating in your bones.

Permission Granted.

STEP TWO
SET THE INVITATION

THE INVITATION IS THE ACT OF CALLING UPON YOUR supernatural inspirations to help guide you in your journey. It is a deeply personal summoning of the Spirits to request their help with something they excelled at in their lifetime.

Have you ever wondered what it would be like to invite Andy Warhol to a midnight tea? Or sip some cognac with Louis Armstrong while you play jazz until sunrise? Or paint your life story alongside Frida Kahlo in her studio? When you set the Invitation, you're inviting a supernatural guide to help you with your spell.

You never perform a spell alone, even if you're the only one visible. When you cast a spell, you are inviting a supernatural force to engage with you in your quest.

As Witches of Spectaculus, we live with the veil between the worlds of the living and the dead slightly parted. The Invitation allows us to commune on a personal, raw level with the Spirits and the Ancestors. We work together with them on a spell. They aren't seen as some distant entity that is a far reach away from us. Their knowledge, inspiration, and creative genius are waiting to be shared. Invite them. Entice them. Honor them.

SETTING THE INVITATION, STEP BY STEP

1. **Set Your Intention.** What is the purpose of your spell? Set a
   clear intention of what you want this spell to accomplish in one
   focused sentence and write that sentence in your grimoire.
   Example: "The intention of this spell is to stir up my creativity
   and focus to write a book."

2. **Choose Your Guide.** Who would best guide you from the
   Otherside for this spell? Think about your heroes, people who
   have inspired you, and people who have already carved out the
   path that you wish to walk.

   If I want inspiration and confidence in my writing, I call on
   Jack Kerouac, Saint of the Open Road. In *Visions of Cody*, he
   wrote, "I am writing this book because we are all going to die."
   Even now, as I type these words, that sentence of Kerouac's
   drives me. Through the Invitation, he has helped me write the
   book you are holding in your hands.

   Once you have chosen your guide, write the following
   sentence, incorporating their name in your grimoire: "I choose
   _____ as my supernatural guide for this spell."

3. **Prepare Your Ritual Space.** Think of preparing the ritual space
   for your supernatural guest like having someone you want to
   impress over for tea. In fact, an old Bohemian tradition was to
   serve tea immediately to guests upon their arrival, the thinking
   being that giving someone a drink of hospitality right away
   makes them more likely to act in your favor.

   Customize the experience of the Invitation for your esteemed
   supernatural guest. Evoke the power of the senses: taste, touch,
   smell, sound, and sight. Light candles, dim the lights, throw some
   incense that you think they'd dig on the cauldron. Go through
   your record collection and pull out something appropriate.
   Remember that your guide has left clues to help you summon
   them, perhaps through the art, writing, and other creative outlets
   they left behind. Your ritual space should welcome your guide.

Jack Kerouac mused about flickering candles melting down the sides of empty wine bottles from the previous night's revelry. He created a musical poem accompanied by jazz about his love and admiration for Charlie Parker. He wrote his novels on a typewriter with a single long scroll of paper. To decorate my ritual space where I call on him as my guide, I drag out my old 1968 typewriter and place his picture on the keys. I light a yellow candle to signify the color of the lines in the open road and place the burning candle in the mouth of an empty wine bottle. I put on a Charlie Parker record to have the sweet saxophone summon Kerouac.

In your grimoire, write down this heading: "Creative Ways to Decorate My Ritual Space for My Supernatural Guide, _____." Below it, write down some ideas that are relevant to your guide. Do research, pick your three favorites, gather your supplies, and adorn your ritual space in an alluring way that will catch your guide's eye.

4. **Make an Offering.** What are thoughtful personal gifts that will attract your supernatural guest? Entice them to be your guide with at least three personal tributes. Honor them by offering their favorite drink, scents, delicacies, songs, objects, and/or vices. The more energy you put into considering these tributes, the more energy you will receive from your invited guest. Light your creative fire with thoughtful offerings.

I'd set out a shot of tequila, which was Kerouac's favorite drink. He loved eating Chinese takeout from white cardboard containers, so I might order up some pan-fried chop suey for him. His writing romanticized ground travel—by train, by car, by bus, and by foot. A ticket stub from a bus or a train trip, a key chain for a 1949 Hudson he talks about driving in *On the Road*, or a pair of men's shoes in size 11 for Jack's wanderings—all of these would work as offerings.

In your grimoire, write down your offering as follows: "An offering that I would like to give to my supernatural guide _____ is _____."

5. **Be Open to Connection.** The Spirits will come through in dreams, in flashes of electric inspiration, in synchronicity, and in signs. Hold them close. Leave a picture of your chosen guide out and light a candle every time you are working toward making your spell manifest. Thank them when they come through. Get ready to have the most dynamic supernatural force ready to guide you. Make sure to log any signs, dreams, or strange coincidences that happen into your grimoire.

STEP THREE
Uncover Your Bones

ADDING THE BONES IS THE POWERFUL ACT OF INFUSING your artistic essence into your spells. Art and Witchcraft are legendary lovers, and when we use our Bones—our creative expression and art that makes us unique—and let them rise to the surface, we bring ourselves to a different state of being, a higher vibe of hypnotic, revolutionary magick.

To uncover your own Bones, ask yourself:

> **How do I like to creatively express myself?**

In your grimoire, write down the heading, "The Bones." Below that, write down all of the ways in which you creatively express yourself. You can return to this list for each new spell that you concoct to look for innovative ways to add your Bones.

For instance, if your creative talents include writing poetry or playing music, you can use this in your spells to sing or recite your own magickal incantations. If you like to make jewelry or sew or knit clothing, you can enchant the objects you make with the spell's intention, like sewing a cloak for confidence or creating a bottle necklace with spells for love sealed inside. If you like to cook or garden, think about stirring the intention of your community-building spell into a batch of cookies to feed to your friends and neighbors, or plant your spell of abundance in rich soil with seeds that will bloom and grow. If you like to paint, draw, or take photos, consider using these art forms to produce a visual picture of what you want to manifest in your spell.

The act of stirring our creative Bones sets our minds in a dreamy, imaginative place that goes hand in hand with the mindset we need to birth our most powerful spells. We are Witches of Spectaculus, after all, where our creative mojo reigns supreme. Tap into your own artful Bones and infuse them into your spells.

Our Bones are tarot and rock and roll.

STEP FOUR
Add Your Sorcery Signature

Jimi, 1967

WELCOME TO THE GRITTY, HARDCORE SIDE OF MAGICK. I'm talking about *the* power boost for spells that you'll never see on a rickety wooden shelf in the most badass Witch shop in Salem.

Your Sorcery Signature is your hair, nails, saliva, blood, and teeth. It is what you add to magnetize a spell to you. Think of it this way: your spell is a letter you send for the Spirits to read. Your powerfully unique DNA is your one-of-a-kind signature. Adding your Sorcery Signature is adding your physical essence—the very pieces you're made of—to your spell.

Squeamish? Sure. Maybe. But remember that you're learning Witchcraft from a burlesque girl whose wedding ring is made from her husband's tooth that was extracted when he was thirteen. I've got the very essence, the teenage bones of the man I love, on my fire finger that connects to my heart.

Don't let the Sorcery Signature make you queasy. It is part of you.

```
Witchcraft Rule No. 1:
Never be afraid of your own power.
```

The power of using a Sorcery Signature is undeniable. In my lifetime, I have woven strands of my hair with my husband's and hid it in the roots of a knotty old sacred tree in New Orleans in a love spell that had us both smitten and drunk on each other. I have tied strands of my hair around my chihuahua's collar when she was away from me so I could keep her energetically close. I painted a tiny magickal symbol with my own menstrual blood for a dream I wanted to birth, and within eight weeks it was mine. My body houses vibrant, earth-shattering power. *So does yours.*

Niney, Queen Wolf of the Witches & Me

East River, NYC

For the spells in this book, spells you create on your own, or any other spells you find to perform, take a moment to find a space in the spell where you can add your chosen Sorcery Signature.

Here are some options and ideas to add your Sorcery Signature. Your spells will be more powerful if there's an element of you in them. You can also use my incantation suggestions to "announce" your Sorcery Signature to the spell and the Spirits.

HAIR

Hair taken from the crown of your head or your pubic area will amplify your spell. If you are doing a love spell with your beloved, ask for a strand of their hair to braid so you can braid the two together. You can also keep a piece of each other's hair in a locket over your heart.

Incantation suggestion:

"I add to this spell a strand of my hair as a magnet of magick to find me anywhere."

One of my earliest childhood memories was staring at "The Nixy" from The Yellow Fairy Book by Andrew Lang. I was enchanted by her magickal hair.

NAILS

Your fingernails are the tips of your personal magick wands—your fingers! When you point, you are directing energy toward something you want or wish to draw others' attention to. Imagine that powerful energy: just by pointing your finger, you've commanded all eyes to focus. As part of your being, like hair, fingernail clippings can be used to amplify purpose in your spell.

Incantation suggestion:

"Crescent moon clippings from the tips of my fingers, in every spell cast my essence lingers."

SALIVA

Saliva acts as the seal of your word and speaking your truth in spells. In Bohemian lore, pacts were sealed by both parties spitting on their own hands and then pressing their palms together in a shake. Saliva magick says: "This is my word."

Incantation suggestion:

"Breath of life and dew from my tongue, I speak it, I say it, my will is done."

BLOOD

Blood acts as the life-giving flow of your being. We've all heard of the rock-and-roll romantics who carry glass vials of each other's blood dangling from silver rope chains around their necks. Pricking your finger and putting a single drop of your own blood on a magickal amulet of yours or other magickal tools will bring them to life. Using menstrual blood in spells helps birth new opportunities, new love, and new visions.

Incantation suggestion:

"Drop of blood, pulse vibrant and red, act as the needle weaving magickal thread. Sew my intention into the story of my days, I summon my desire with my own Witchy ways."

TEETH

Teeth are for rare, deeply personal enchantments, as they are part of our skeleton. Teeth can be used as charms or talismans to bond deeply with another person or creature. Wearing the teeth of someone you love keeps their energy and love near you.

Incantation suggestion:

"I add my teeth, my magickal bits of bone, a piece of the skeleton that I call my home."

STEP FIVE:

RAISING ENERGY AND CASTING IT OUT

ONCE YOU FEEL LIKE A SPELL IS COMPLETE, YOU MUST cast it out for the Spirits to help work it with you. Think of a spell as writing a letter to the Spirits: Steps One through Four are the equivalent of getting a paper and pen, writing the letter, putting it in an envelope, and sealing it and putting a stamp on it. If you don't do Step Five—raising and casting the energy out—you've left that letter on your desk! You need to take it to the mailbox and drop it in, babe!

Raising and casting the energy for your spell—in other words, communicating it to the Spirits—is the final step. You pull all your magick together in one final exaltation to cast out your energy, to thank and bid farewell to your guide and the Spirits with one final thrust of your hands to the sky, a clap, an exuberant howl, or even speaking the Spectaculus words of closure in a loud and powerful voice: "See it. Be it. So be it."

For the final step of most of my spells, rituals, ceremonies, I use the Wishing Circle, an old Bohemian tradition taught to me by my Grandma Helen. The Wishing Circle is the most powerful way I know to raise and charge energy toward what you want to manifest. The Wishing Circle focuses on the purpose of your spell, uses your breath to give it life, and the friction of rubbing your palms together to raise powerful energy for your spellcasting. The ritual as I perform it that melds the Bohemian traditions I learned from my Grandma Helen and my own ritual creations. Ignite your casting power through this cherished ritual! Here are the seven steps.

1. **Think of a Wish.** Think of a wish that you would like to conjure into reality. If you are doing a solo spell, state in one positive sentence what you want the spell to accomplish. If you are working with a Coven or a large group of people, ask them to think of their own individual wishes but not say them out loud. You can also choose to do a powerful group working where everyone has the same wish.

2. **Visualize the Wish Coming True.** Close your eyes and visualize your intention manifesting into reality. Feel it. See the details of it. What does the air smell like around you? Is it night or day? What are you wearing? Who is there? What do you hear around you? What colors or objects do you see? Craft the world with your mind. Conjure the outcome of your spell with a clear vision in your mind.

3. **Enliven the Wish with Your Breath.** Cup your hands in front of you as if you were going to hold water in them. Imagine the curving lines of your palms holding your stories. See your vision in your mind and blow it into your cupped hands. This is the practice of blowing "life" into your wish and giving it oxygen. In Bohemian lore, you are using your breath and your thoughts to write that new story upon the lines on your hands.

Dancing with the spirits of the CHELSEA HOTEL, NYC.

4. **Build Energy for the Spell.** Clasp your hands shut, palm-to-palm in a prayer position. Rapidly move your palms back and forth against each other to cause heat and friction. This practice is raising the energy of your vision, building heat to sear it into your life story. Grandma Helen called this act of building energy "cooking up your palms." Continue to do this until you feel your hands burning hot with intention and surging with power, dear Witch!

5. **Charge the Spell with Energy and Cast the Spell.** You can choose to use this supernatural energy to cast a spell (option a), to charge up objects or items you make (option b), or to connect with an entire group to raise energy and cast it out in a spell (option c).

    a. **If you are raising energy to cast a spell alone.** Once your hands are burning with hot energy, press your open palms against your heart. Close your eyes and breathe deeply. You will feel a hot surge of energy soar through you. This is your intention and vision igniting in your being.

    b. **If you are raising energy to charge your intention into an object (an amulet, a bag, a dream pillow, a carved candle, a potion bottle).** Rub your hands together until they are burning hot, then clasp the object between your palms. Close your eyes and feel the electric energy from your palms charging up the object.

    c. **If you are raising energy to conduct a spell as a group.** Stand in a circle. Everyone should rub their hands together until they are so hot they feel like they are burning. As a group, count to three slowly out loud. On three, everyone should extend their palms to the side so that each person's palms are pressed to the palm of the people on either side of them. The group should then close their eyes and take three deep breaths. You will feel the energy flow around the circle, raising the overall power.

6. **Show Gratitude.** If you are alone, extend your arms all the way up like you are reaching for the sky. Your fingertips should be held straight up, with your palms facing outward in front of you, as if you are a human Y. If you are in a group, continue to stand in a circle palm to palm, then raise your arms up to the sky together.

> Thank the Spirits, Ancestors, and Guides for their help.
>
> If you are in a group, thank the people who put their energy into the circle.
>
> Send the force of the positive energy out through your fingertips to all of our brothers and sisters across the world who need the magick.

7. **Send It to the Sky.** Hold your own hands out in front of you, palms up and side by side, as if you were making a platform on which a small invisible messenger bird stands. Count to three and blow the spirit bird up into the sky. Imagine that the bird carries your vision so that it soars out into the universe, reaching the highest points of the heavens!

Maeve, Sage, and Me.
CHELSEA HOTEL, NYC.

Finally, here are two important things to remember:

ALLOW THE MAGICK TO DO ITS WORK.

Oftentimes when you cast a spell, you want instant results.
The trick is to cast out the spell and not obsess over it or question
your spellwork. Casting a spell is like casting a line to catch a fish;
you let the line go and then you sit quietly and wait until you
get a sign that your fish is on the hook. You would never catch
a fish if you cast the line and then kept obsessively, repeatedly
reeling it back in, checking the empty line, casting it out, and
reeling it back in. When you cast a spell and let it go, you are
demonstrating that you trust your magick, you trust your Wild,
and you believe that all will unfold for the very best.

SPELLS ARE THE COMBINATION OF INTENTION AND ACTION.

Intention and action make a spell work. When you cast a spell and use only intention without action, it is like standing frozen six feet away from those sensor doors at the supermarket, waiting for them to open—but nothing happens. In other words, if you cast a spell, you then must do some work to help get results. If you are looking for a true love, for example, cast the spell to magnetize the right person to you, then make an active effort to meet people. Intention creates a magick vision, and action amplifies it, helping to make the vision real.

HOW *to* USE *the* MOON *in* SPELLCASTING

The moon is our nightly reminder of the sacred and the mystical. She is our lighthouse in the celestial sky, an ancient teacher and guide. Each of Her phases holds unique power, symbolism, and signs. When performing a spell, always consider the phase of the moon in order to optimize it! Call on Her when it is time and She will answer!

NEW MOON

The new moon signifies a fresh start. This is the time to perform spells that encourage new beginnings. Cast spells for calling in a new love, a new health program, or a new home, project, or idea.

FULL MOON

The full moon is Queen of the Night! Channel this peak energy to raise your supernatural instincts by charging your Witchcraft tools in Her potent light and gather moon water by setting out a bowl of water to use in spells and moon baths to amplify power.

WAXING MOON

The waxing moon is about growth. As the moon builds in the sky, you can harness that power in spells for things you want to build. This is the time to cast spells for abundance, notoriety, love, energy, growth, and luck.

WANING MOON

When the moon wanes, it is a time of letting go. As the moon disappears in the sky, cast spells to clear away obstacles, clean out or organize your home, or let go of old behavior or relationships. It is also an excellent time to look inward, to reflect and work on your intuition or divination skills.

OPTIMAL DAYS *for* CASTING SPELLS

Each day of the week has a secret held in its name that aligns it with certain magickal properties that can help you optimize your spellcasting. Sunday is the "sun's day," so it makes sense that it is a day of casting spells for happiness, joy, and playful creativity. Similarly, Monday is the "moon's day," so it's a good time to do spells that align you with the moon's mysterious affiliations: intuition, dreamwork, and connecting to the Otherside. Here's a list for the week in full.

DAY	RULER	RECOMMENDED SPELLWORK
Sunday	Sun	Spells for happiness, joy, childlike inspiration, creativity
Monday	Moon	Spells for heightening intuition, dreams and divination, and for connecting to family or friends on the Otherside
Tuesday	Mars	Spells for standing in your power, taking action, success
Wednesday	Mercury	Spells for adventure, communication and education, wisdom, and knowledge
Thursday	Jupiter	Spells for abundance, good luck, and good health
Friday	Venus	Spells for love, beauty, sex magick, and self-love
Saturday	Saturn	Spells for protection and for letting go

How to Write Your Own Spells

WITHOUT A DOUBT, SOME OF THE VERY BEST spells are ones that you write yourself. Here's how to use Spectaculus Spellcasting to craft a spell that's truly potent because it includes your unique and powerful Witchy spark!

When you are writing your own spell, it will be more powerful if you allow yourself a few days to plan it out. After all, you are getting ready for a sacred ceremony and summoning the supernatural to you! The thought, time, and creativity you put into your spell writing will exponentially increase its power—definitely worth your while!

Here are some tips to get the best spellcasting results:

Define the purpose of the spell in a single focused sentence. Before you cast any spell, you must be very clear about why you want to cast it and what result you hope to achieve. Just as you enter your destination into your GPS when you're taking a road trip, you need to know where you want to go before you start driving. The first thing you should do is write down the purpose of your spell in one focused sentence. Examples might be: "My efforts are noticed at work and I receive a promotion." "I am confident in my singing voice and I easily find the right band to join and sing my heart out." "My new home is a peaceful place filled with creativity, joy, and friends." Notice how I did not "wish" or "hope" or "want" anything—my sentence was structured as if I had already obtained my desire. You want to be making an empowered, fulfilled statement.

Decide how you want to set the Invitation. A high school friend used to call me "the ghostess with the mostess" because I loved to prepare my bedroom for the Spirits. The walls were covered from floor to ceiling with pictures cut from glossy magazines of the people on the Otherside who had inspired me and who I wanted to connect

with for guidance and inspiration. I would shut off the lights and play an isolated vocal track of Nirvana's "Smells Like Teen Spirit" starting at 0:43 seconds to hear Kurt Cobain call out "Hello" repeatedly in my dark room so I could invite him in.

Set up for the supernatural party, sweet Witch! Give yourself plenty of time to get any supplies you need or to set up your ritual space. Have fun and enjoy this process! Don't rush it.

Use your creative skills in the spell. Think about the Bones, babe. How do you want to express yourself in a creative way for the particular purpose of this spell? Do you want to write your own rhyming incantation to sing or speak under the appropriate moon phase? Create a collage of the things you want to manifest in the spell? Make an amulet to weave your intention into magickal jewelry created by your own hands? Make a meal and stir the contents, speaking your intentions over them? Paint a picture blindfolded and let the Spirits speak through you? Take your time to come up with something that feels right.

Align the timing of the spell with the optimal moon phase. Refer to "How to Use the Moon in Spellcasting" on page 60, then select an appropriate date to cast your spell. Setting a date in advance treats spellcasting like an important ceremonial event. It's a special date, something to prepare for and put energy into, which helps you build your own power as a Witch and boosts the power of your spells exponentially.

SPELLCASTING
A Case Study

SO NOW YOU'VE DONE ALL YOUR PREPARATION WORK, your spellcasting date on the calendar has arrived, and the moon is in a favorable phase. Let's say you've determined the goal of the spell is that you want to increase warmth and passion with your partner. Your sentence of intention might be: "My relationship with my partner is filled with warmth and passion." Here's how you'd perform the spell step by step:

WRITE THE PERMISSION SLIP

This is a love spell, so you need to believe that you deserve the warmth and passion you are asking for. Write a Permission Slip that allows you to step into the most romantic part of your being, the part that bans negativity and excuses from your thinking by focusing intensely on what you desire and why you deserve it. A Permission Slip for this spell might look like this:

I give myself full, unrestrained permission to let my own wild passion flow through me and set sparks of warmth and excitement into my relationship. I do this because I give myself permission to live a FULL life of juiciness, and as a magic-maker I do not settle for less. I deserve to have delicious warmth and passion in my relationship and so does my partner. By taking the time and energy to cast this spell, I am already raising the connection between us.

I create with my word. I speak spells into existence. I weave my destiny with all the love, power, and divinity that courses through the blood in my veins.

See it. Be it. So be it.

65

CIRCE the SORCERESS

SET THE INVITATION

In the preparation above, you've determined who you would like to invite to help you in this love spell. For this example, let's say it's your deceased grandparents, who had a sweet romantic relationship. Now is the time to set up an altar (see page 234) to call them in by placing on it the objects you gathered or special things they liked. You might put a picture of them together in the center of your altar with a lit candle in an empty bottle of their favorite red wine. You might put on the song they danced to at their wedding and then perhaps lay Grandpa's favorite cigar and Grandma's favorite red lipstick on the altar. Now it's time to invite them over.

Greet them. Talk to them out loud. It might feel silly at first, but it helps a lot to talk things out. After speaking to them a short while, the energy in the room will shift—you will feel it, and your words will start to flow more easily. Get personal, dear Witch, let them know why you chose them to help you in this spell. In this example, perhaps you'd say that you were always inspired by their relationship and you're looking for their help to spark that sweet warmth and connection in your own union.

ADD YOUR BONES

Decide how you are going to use a creative talent in the spell. In the preparation, you've thought about this and made the decision about how you want this spell to take form. So, if you're looking to ignite warmth and passion in your relationship, how would you express that? Say you're really into crafting and you love to knit. You've decided that knitting a scarf that you make with your own hands for your partner is the perfect shape that this spell will take. Or you might knit a tiny red heart that you will sew into your lover's pillowcase so that they can rest their head on your love every night.

ADD YOUR SORCERY SIGNATURE

Here's where things get interesting and ramp up to the next level! Your creative Bones and your Sorcery Signature go hand in hand. They are the Spectaculus Spellcasting version of peanut butter and jelly—a winning combination! Let's say you decided that your creative Bones for this spell will be a scarf you knit or a small heart you knit and sew into your lover's pillow. Now you get to decide which Sorcery Signature would be best to include in your creation.

For this example, I'm going to give you two ideas. For the scarf, I'd suggest enchanting it with your Sorcery Signature by knitting in a strand, or even a few strands, of your hair so your lover will always be close to you. You can do the same for the tiny heart on the pillow, or you could add a drop of your own blood (menstrual or a tiny pinprick from your thumb) and put it on the back of the heart so it is hidden. That way, your blood and life-force energy will be within the heart you made.

As a Witch, you're bringing these things to life with your Sorcery Signature. As you are adding the elements of hair or blood to the Bones of the spell, you can use the suggested incantation for hair and blood on pages 52–53, which you will say out loud in a powerful voice to ignite the power.

RAISING ENERGY AND CASTING IT OUT

In this example, you would use the wishing circle ritual to charge this object you knitted with magick. Take a moment and think of your partner, imagine increased warmth and passion in your relationship. How does it feel? Let yourself daydream about this. Once you feel it and can see it clearly in your mind, cup your hands in front of you and blow that vision into your palms. Then press your palms together in a prayer position and rub back and forth to build friction and heat.

When your hands are so hot with energy that you can't handle it anymore, grab the scarf you made and hold it in your hands. Feel all that energy of your vision and your wish flow from your palms into the scarf. You are now magickally charging the scarf and casting an enchanted spell on it. Here is the moment that you might want to try your hand at writing your own rhyming incantations and saying them, or you can just say your intention out loud:

> This magickal scarf knitted by my hands and entwined with my hair fills my partner with feelings of the sweet warmth and passion we have together. Our passion, warmth, and deep connection for each other thrives and flourishes with every passing day!

To finish your spell, send it off with the Spectaculus casting command:

> See it. Be it. So be it.

Sigil Magick

IMAGINE YOU'RE WRITING A LOVE LETTER FOR THE first time to someone you are really hot for. You find a beautiful piece of paper, something that feels worthy of your words. You carefully craft your words in jet-black ink that swirls with the curves of your sensual handwriting. You go through an emotional process as you write, and the passion and the excitement of sending out the letter moves you. You are casting that electrifying love energy you are feeling into the words. That letter hums with energy; it's a love entity that you imbued with life—and believe me, when your lover receives it, they feel it!

And that, dear Witch, is exactly the magick that lies in a sigil. It's like a secret love letter you write in the shape of a symbol and send to the Spirits with the hope that they will support your intentions. A sigil is a one-of-a-kind symbol that you create to represent a specific magickal purpose. Think of a sigil as a spell in the form of a symbol rather than in words.

Sigils work by bypassing the conscious mind and diving straight into your subconscious. The conscious mind is where all our naysaying doubts and fears live, so if we can bypass the conscious mind, we can also bypass those doubts and fears!

Imagine seeing the word "peace." If you're having a bad day, your conscious mind processes that word and you might have a negative thought like, peace isn't possible. Now imagine you see a peace symbol. Its meaning connects directly with your subconscious mind, bypassing your conscious mind so you don't question its intention. The peace symbol goes into your brain with its original pure intention and meaning: "Peace." Sigils affect our brains the same way symbols do.

You can find sigils that have been designed and charged with a particular meaning, but it is far more powerful to design your own! It's like the difference between buying a greeting card and just signing your name versus making a card and filling it with your personal emotions and thoughts. Yes, they accomplish the same result, but the handmade one is more powerful, connected, and meaningful.

HOW TO CREATE a SIGIL
· and ·
SPECTACULUS SIGIL SONGS

LEAN IN A LITTLE BIT CLOSER, MY DARLING WITCH.
Grab your grimoire and get ready to take notes, because not only am
I going to show you how to create sigils step by step, but I am also
going to reveal a powerful magick technique that has not been written
or shared anywhere else in the world—until now.

This technique is my very own magick invention, and I call it the
Spectaculus Sigil Song.

The Spectaculus Sigil Song is an enchantment. The word "enchantment" is derived from the Latin *incantare*, meaning to "enchant with
song," and this spell does just that. This technique drastically increases
the power of your sigils and amplifies your manifestation power through
a magickal melody that is all your own!

Behold now and enter the world of sigils and the secret enchantment
power of the Spectaculus Sigil Song!

TOOLS AND MATERIALS

+ **Your grimoire**
+ **Black pen**

+ **Hand drum** *(optional)*

Le ton ma lou Je porte
Vient me le au
me le et le six
SAIGNANTE LOU M'A PERCÉ
CHE te
den
air su
ne su fleg

The French poet
Guillaume Apollinaire
was famous for his
calligrams (a piece of
writing that is arranged
on the page so that it forms
a thematically related
shape).

Here, whether you
speak French or not,
the meaning is clear:

Je t'adore!

CAST THE SPELL

1. Begin by writing down your magickal purpose in one word or one clear sentence on a piece of paper. For this example, let's make a statement for a sigil with the magickal purpose of evoking feelings of power and confidence as a Witch. The example sentence is:

I am a powerful and confident Witch.

2. Take your pen and circle all the vowels (A, E, I, O, U) in your magickal intention; they are not part of the sigil you will make, as sigils are formed only with consonants. In this example, you would circle the vowels and set them aside for later when you create your sigil song. They appear in this order:

I am a powerful and confident Witch.

I a a o e u a o i e i

3. Now focus solely on the consonants, as that is how you will create your sigil. With the consonants that you have in your magickal intention sentence, rewrite your sentence "I am a powerful and confident Witch" as if the vowels were invisible.

I am a powerful and confident Witch.

M p w r f l n d c n f d n t w t c h

4. From that list of consonants, break it down so that each consonant is represented only once. In this instance, the letter c is repeated twice, as are the letters n and t.

M p w r f l n d c n f d n t w t c h

M p w r f l n d c t h

5. Now is the time to make your sigil—and to get creative! Take a clean piece of paper and play with the letters. Always keep at least one letter connected to the others. You can merge the letters together or turn them upside down or sideways. You can make a letter upper or lower case or big or small on the page. You can add flourishes like dots, waves of light, spirals, or stars around the outside of the sigil. Take your time and play with different options until you land on something that feels powerful to you. One of the coolest things about this form of magick is that the sigil you make will be unique. I often try the letters in several combinations and various flourishes in various configurations. I keep working on the sigil until I feel I have the most powerful representation of my intention.

Here is a sigil I created for our example statement, "I am a powerful and confident Witch."

6. Now you must imbue this mystical symbol with energy to give it life. Focus on the sigil and repeat this incantation three times in a strong and clear voice:

Sigil Sorcery born in this hour,
Magick symbol imbued with power.
Secret alphabet in a seal fulfill,
The fullest potential of my
purest will.

7. The final step is to craft your own unique Spectaculus Sigil Song. To do this, you will be taking the vowels you circled from your magickal purpose statement in step 2 and singing them back into the written sigil to imbue it with life. When you use your voice to sing the vowels back into the sigil, you give it life through the oxygen of your breath and the song itself. Singing vowels evokes something primal and ancient in our beings. A Spectaculus Sigil Song voiced sounds like something our Ancestors long ago would have sung around a bonfire.

The vowels taken from this example are:

```
I a a o e u a o i e i
```

Tap out a heartbeat rhythm on the floor, your thighs, or a drum. Look at the sigil as you sing this line of vowels three times. When you sing, hold each vowel for a moment before going into the next one. (For instance, the start of this Sigil Song would sound like: "iiiiiiiiiiiiiiiiiii ayyyyyyyyyyyyyyyy ayyyyyyyyyyy ohhhhhhhhhh.")

Don't judge your singing! Let your Wild flow and tap into that primal part of you. Let the vowel sounds come out of your mouth and enchant the sigil with your own potent and powerful one-of-a-kind song!

WHERE TO PLACE SIGILS

I put sigils anywhere that will remind me of the purpose of my magick spell. The energy and life you imbue into a sigil are captured within it in almost the same way a photograph can capture the magick of a special moment in your life. Every time that you look upon a sigil you've created and imbued with purpose, it will fill you with its energy and remind you of your powerful intention.

Use your imagination when placing your sigil; put it somewhere it will help you the most. You might paint a sigil for health on the tops of your workout sneakers so you can look down and gain power from it. You might draw a sigil for confidence on your arms like a mystical tattoo. You could even etch a sigil for your protection in chalk on the walkway to your front door.

The sigil I made for our example "I am a powerful and confident Witch" would be perfect to decorate my grimoire, cauldron, broom, and other magickal tools. I could write it on a small piece of cloth and sew it onto my magickal red velvet cape. A sigil is your own secret symbol that is there to mirror that power to you any time you need it.

Candle Magick

ANDLE MAGICK WAS EXTREMELY POPULAR IN Bohemian culture, partly because it was readily available and easy to do. You could take any type of candle, carve your magick intention on it in the form of words, a symbol, a sigil, or a combination of all three, then strike a match to set it afire for a powerful spell. Grandma Helen believed that when you light a candle, the good Spirits can find you and help you with your magickal wish.

Just as lighthouse beams cast their glow into the darkness to help ships find their way to shore, a candle that you've carved beams energy to you when you need it. When you craft magick with your own hands, the spell becomes more personal and potent.

A Lighthouse Candle is a powerful spell full of intention and artistic decisions that are uniquely yours. Choose a clear one-sentence purpose for your spell. The sigil, symbol, or word you choose to carve into the candle represents the essence of what you want your spell to achieve. Then, based upon your spell's purpose, choose a candle color, an essential oil, and glitter that correspond to that intention. The color of the glitter should be in keeping with the vibe you want to sprinkle onto your magickal purpose. (See my note about candle safety on the opposite page.) For instance, if you choose red for a love candle, how about gold glitter sprinkled on your design to give you that boost of happiness and joy for your love spell? Each aspect of this candle has a purpose that you custom design! Finish by setting your Sorcery Signature into the candle to amplify its power to you.

When you light the wick of this candle, you cannot help but be blown away by the beauty that you crafted into the spell through the candle-making process. This is one of the favorite crafting spell projects at Witch Camp, because after camp is over and we all go home to our places in the world, we still have our Lighthouse Candles that we can burn whenever we need a reminder to focus on the magickal intention with which we crafted the candle.

You can make Lighthouse Candles for any purpose—love, abundance, confidence building, house blessings, you name it. Refer to the Spectaculus Color Magick Chart on page 78 to choose a candle color that's aligned with the intention of your spell and a complementary glitter color to boost your magick! If you're having trouble choosing color for glitter, gold or silver is a good choice: both always add some supernatural sass to a spell. The Spectaculus Essential Oils Magick Chart on page 79 will help you choose the right essential oil to boost your intention. Now you've got everything you need to get started.

USE NONTOXIC, SAFE-BURNING CANDLES IF YOU CAN

Even though lead has been banned from use in candle wicks since 2003, some wicks have a metal core that contains lead and other toxins that release as the candle burns. Sometimes you can see the metal, but not always, so err on the side of caution and buy nontoxic, safe-burning candles.

Here are a few tips:

Look for a 100 percent cotton wick or cherry wood. Don't buy a candle with a wick that's too large for the container you're using, as this can create a lot of heat and produce excessive soot and residue.

Look for candles made of 100 percent clean-burning soy wax or beeswax, as both paraffin- and petroleum-based waxes release chemicals when burned. Check the label carefully, as many candles are made of a mix of paraffin and other waxes. It's also a good idea to buy sustainably sourced and naturally derived candles, if you can.

If you want a fragrant candle, add your own essential oils. Buy a candle without fragrance. It's safer. You don't know what you're getting when the label on the side lists "fragrance" as an ingredient. Spectaculus Witches add their own 100 percent naturally derived essentials.

SPECTACULUS COLOR MAGICK CHART

Colors speak to us on a subconscious level and have a magick language all their own. Here are some helpful color associations for your magickal workings. You can use color magick in anything, from your color choice of an outfit for a special occasion to your magick candles and the glitter you decorate them with, from the cloth that you spread over your altar to the color of your bedroom!

	Red	Love, passion, and romance
	Pink	Self-love and friendship
	Orange	Drawing praise, notice, and attention to you and opening communication
	Yellow	Sunshine energy! Happiness and joy
	Purple	Standing in your power, strong sensual mojo *(no wonder Prince's favorite color was purple!)*
	Blue	Peace, dream magick, and healing
	Green	Abundance and growth
	Black	Deep wisdom, Ancestor magick, and protection
	White	New beginnings, projects, and ideas

Smell is our strongest sense for evoking memory. A whiff of a scent can draw you back to a place or time. The scent of vanilla might bring warm memories of your mother's kitchen when she made you cookies when you were little, or the scent of coconut might evoke the memory of putting on suntan lotion and carefree days at the beach.

Scent is highly emotional and works its own magick. Here are some suggestions for the scents and what they might stir in you to enhance your spells. I recommend using 100 percent naturally derived essential oils.

Citrus oil (grapefruit, orange, lemon, lime)	Happiness and joy
Sandalwood or jasmine oil	Love, sex, and romance
Peppermint oil	Drawing energy, notoriety, and abundance to you
Lavender or cedarwood oil	Calm and inner peace
Bergamot oil	Self-love and friendship
Frankincense oil	Wisdom

- One seven-day pull-out candle in a glass container
- Carving tool (any clay carving tool, pencil, or small pocketknife)
- Nine drops essential oil
- Large glass bowl
- Latex gloves *(optional)*
- Two ounces nontoxic metal glitter
- Measuring teaspoon
- One teaspoon honey, agave, or maple syrup
- One teaspoon sandalwood-based powdered incense or a stick of sandalwood incense
- Lighter

CAST THE SPELL

1. **Set the Intention.** What are you creating a Lighthouse Candle for? Write a sentence declaring its purpose in your grimoire.

2. **Choose the Color of the Candle and Complementary Glitter.** Color has a deep effect on our subconscious. Choose a candle color that best represents your intention and a complementary color for the glitter. Refer to the Spectaculus Color Magick Chart on page 78.

3. **Carve the Candle.** With your carving tool, start about one inch below the top of the candle and etch your name vertically down the side. Next, decide what would represent your intention best: a word, a relevant symbol (heart, sun, moon), a picture, or a magickal sigil. Lightly carve the shape into the candle to outline it. You can work freehand or use stencils. Make sure you always go back over your design once you are satisfied with it to carve the lines deeply so that the glitter can sink into the grooves when you decorate it in step 5.

4. **Dress the Candle with Essential Oil.** The proper way to anoint a candle is by leaning the candle on its side with the design facing up. Place nine drops of oil onto the candle. Take both of your palms and wrap your hands around the candle and rub the oil into all the grooves in an up-and-down motion.

5. **Adorn the Candle.** After you have oiled the candle, hold it over a large bowl and sprinkle a generous amount of glitter all over the design of the candle. You can use a damp paper towel or latex gloves to wipe the glitter off and into the grooves in a wringing motion, or you can just do what our Witch Camp sister Kristi does: wipe off the glitter with your bare hands and then wildly rub all the excess glitter into your hair. It's a look, babe!

6. **Purify the Candle.** Scoop a teaspoon of wood-based powdered incense. Take a lighter and wave it over the incense on the spoon so that it catches fire. Lightly blow out the flame so that the incense is smoking embers. Overturn the incense into the bottom of the empty glass of the candle. The incense smoke will travel up through the glass to purify it for the candle—and it looks like a magick potion steaming from a glass! Alternatively, you can also extend a lit stick of sandalwood incense into the glass and swirl it around so that the glass fills with smoke. Take the glass and "toast" it to the sky, repeating this incantation three times with power:

```
Wick, Wax, Fire Light.
Beacon in the dead of night
Toast the Spirits in the sky
Magick. Spellcast. Multiply.
```

7. **Feed the Candle.** Feeding a magickal candle is an offering to thank the Spirits for their help. My Grandma loved feeding her candles honey to make things "sweet." You can also use agave or maple syrup. Take a tiny bit on a teaspoon, have a taste, then feed the candle by dripping the honey into the base of the empty candle glass.

8. **Add Your Sorcery Signature.** If the candle has a metal disk at the bottom that holds the wick, pry it out with your fingertips and pull the wick out of the bottom of the candle about a half inch. Then wrap a piece of your hair around the wick and push the hair-wrapped wick back up into the candle. You can also put one of your crescent-moon-shaped fingernail clippings inside or even a drop of blood (either menstrual or a pinprick from your thumb). This is a tradition that I created to use my DNA as a magnet at the foundation of the candle. If the candle doesn't have a metal disk at the bottom, I lick my fingertips and swipe the saliva over the top of the wick as a pact of truth. A word of caution: you should only lick the wick.

9. **Light Your Finished Candle and Charge It Up with Grandma Helen's Wishing Circle Technique.** Slide the designed candle back into the glass. Charge the finished Lighthouse Candle with intention by using Grandma Helen's Wishing Circle technique: Close your eyes and visualize the positive outcome that you desire for your spell. See the details. Let your mind roam so that you really feel it happening and coming true. When you are ready, put your cupped hands in front of you and blow your vision into your hands with your breath. Put your palms together in a prayer position and rub them back and forth quickly to cause heat and friction. When the heat and the energy of rubbing your palms together is so intense you can't do it anymore, grab the candle in the container in your hands and hold it. Close your eyes and take three deep breaths. Feel your energy and your intention travel from the palms of your hands into your candle to enchant it. Once you have charged the candle with your intention, light up the wick and watch good things come to you!

PART II

THE
Initiations

WELCOME TO THE FIVE INITIATIONS OF Spectaculus. You have excelled in your supernatural studies in spellcasting, candle magick, and sigil magick. You now hold the knowledge to craft your own original spells and sing the secrets of sigil songs. You stand strong in a long legacy of Bohemian magick, and as you bestow the mysterious, ancient, and powerful word of "Witch" upon yourself, you believe that you have the power to boldly transform and design your own destiny.

Yes. You do.

The Five Initiations of Spectaculus are designed to help you master your magick in the areas of self-love, protection, healing, confidence, manifestation, love, and legacy Witchcraft.

Journey now, dear Witch, through the initiations in the given order. Each initiation expands upon the last as your spellcasting powers, confidence, and supernatural mojo grow! Each initiation begins with a journey that will put you into the magickal mindset necessary for your initiation. Our minds and imaginations are part of our supernatural sorcery, and just as my Grandma Helen trained me, I will walk you through visualizations that will boost your own skills, connection, and deep understanding of the mystical powers you hold within you. Last, in each initiation you will cast three spells, ceremonies, or rituals that will fill you with confidence as you call all the power of your Wild back to you!

Let's begin!

Initiation I

The RESURRECTION of YOUR WILD

I ONCE LIVED IN A LITTLE ONE-HUNDRED-YEAR-OLD cottage on the side of a mountain. I painted it the color of fresh mint and adorned it with delicate wooden gingerbread accents in sky blue and deep purple. This cozy Witch cottage was my safe place in the world, my home.

My own handwritten books of spells sat upon antique shelves painted and peeling. Dried herbs of lavender and rosemary hung from the post-and-beam rafters, and a 1915 mahogany Victrola record player crackled as the ghosts of long-dead musicians sang through its giant horn speaker. My tiny bedroom faced east, the rising sun flooding the room through prism crystals dangling in the windows, creating a kaleidoscope of the colors of morning.

"Home" was a word I had stopped using when I was twelve. That was the year when my Grandma Helen died and my parents' divorce tore our family apart. I lost my sense of home then. I lost my sense of safety, of comfort, of belonging—and didn't find it again until I found the cottage.

One day, while I was doing renovations, I pulled down a layer of rotting wood paneling and stood stunned, for the walls underneath were awash with sapphire blue paint and decorated with gold hand-drawn stars—a 1960s-style night galaxy. In that moment, I felt as if I were staring directly at the backs of the tarot cards my Grandma Helen used when she taught me to read. I knew this was a sign from her. A sign that I was truly, and finally, home.

89

Six years later, I was away for a couple of days for work when I received a call about my house. I wasn't given details, only that I needed to get there immediately. By the time I arrived, ran up the driveway past the red flashing lights of the fire trucks and gawking onlookers, my home was nothing but a charred field of blackness in the shape of things I had loved.

I ducked under the yellow police tape and threw myself on my knees in the toppled black boards and warm ash, clawing at the remains in an attempt to find something, to save anything, to put everything—even one thing—back together. Two firefighters grabbed me by the arms, lifted me up, and carried me to the field by the house. Wailing, I screamed and kicked while they tried to get me to calm down.

"The bells, the bells are by the front door. Get them, get them. Please, please," I sobbed.

There was no front door anymore.

The bells that rang out in magick ceremony for four generations of women in my family were cremated by the flames, never to sing again.

The firefighters said that the fire was most likely caused by old electrical wiring within the walls gone awry or perhaps chewed on by an animal. I could hardly hear anything they said, though. The firemen held me back on the grass, their strong arms on my shoulders, as I told them where to look for things. The treasures were all pure ash: the diary covered in yellow daisies that my Mom wrote for me before I was born; the heart-shaped pin that my Grandpa gave my Grandma on the day they were married; the black-and-white photos of my family's smiling faces from a century ago. I was the self-appointed recordkeeper for my family, the guardian of the physical evidence that proved we existed and of the stories these objects held. Four generations of photos in a psychedelic daisy suitcase in the little library room, now gone. I had assembled a shelf of my favorite childhood books and next to them sat old letters and cards from long-dead family members, each written in unique curving script, destroyed. My family's words were lost to me, transformed into smoke reaching to the sky for the Spirits alone to read. No spell that has ever been wrought would bring them back.

I felt as powerless and as exposed as the burnt skeleton of what once was my home. After the firefighters left, when I started digging around again, trying to recover anything I could recognize, I felt some kind of fight rise in me. The fire had taken my history, but it could not take away my vitality, my magick. It was the one thing I had left.

I knew I needed to do what my Grandma Helen taught me: I needed to cast a candle spell to throw light to dispel my own darkness. And what I'm going to tell you now, what followed a short while after my home was destroyed, is the story of how the spell of the Midnight Library came to be and how you can use this magick to stay connected with and hold onto the very essence of who you are.

The story of the spell begins on a night two months after the fire. A huge bright moon hung low on the mountain; it seemed so close to the earth that I felt I could drive right onto it if I could only find the right road. I was thinking about the road to the moon when, instead of arriving at the temporary home where I was now living, some five miles ahead, I turned my car up the rocky driveway of my lost house instead. I guess I was on autopilot that night because suddenly, there I was, standing in the field where my little cottage once stood. Tall grass had grown up and around the pile of ash, and the only thing left was the flat stone path, a curving invitation to the ghostly place where my old front door once stood.

My mind raced with the spells of my Grandma Helen, as I looked for inspiration, something I could do to feel better, and finally landed on something she'd taught me long ago.

I went back to the car and rifled through a small box of magick items in the trunk that I was transporting from the city to my new temporary home. I grabbed a lighter and a seven-inch candle that would burn for the two-hour experience I needed for this spell. I placed the candle in a mound of dirt where the front door of my home once was. I imagined that with the lighting of that candle, my cottage would appear before me. The crickets were singing loudly in the tall grasses as I lit the wick, and I stood up, as if ready to do battle. With my feet solidly on the ground, my arms held up to the night sky, my Grandma's sapphire ring on my hand flashing as I pointed my fingers like wands to do my bidding,

I commanded my cottage and its magickal contents to appear before me. I sang out to the Spirits. I called to the Ancestors for their help. A force moved through my very bones as they arrived and held me upon their shoulders. I pictured vividly gauzy moonlight beaming through the old windows and casting a glow upon a painted bookshelf. Deep in the spell now, I found myself inside my tiny bedroom, the wall of hand-painted gold stars shining against bright blue. I could hear the faint and scratchy old Victrola in the living room playing Gershwin's "Summertime" from an old 78 record of *Porgy and Bess*. A deep baritone voice sang through the ghost of my home, soothing me and telling me to rise and sing, and I did. I sang out and it gave me the power to continue.

Over the two earthly hours it took for the white candle to burn down at my feet, I moved through the house, gathering objects and pressing them to my heart, as if doing that would pass the power and memory in them onto me. I pictured myself opening my lost diaries and trying to read the words on their pages. I moved my hand in a circular motion to bring the ring of my Grandma's bells into view and sang out to her spirit to help me. I did these things last in my spell as a plea to imprint the words of the memories, of my life, of my books, upon my soul.

I made a deal with myself: when the candle burned down, I had to leave. I would allow myself to walk in the world of the unseen for those two hours only. Then I was once again alone in an empty field of high grass, the cottage I had loved dissipating into the night.

I left the field with a feeling of feverish power in my soul and covered in mosquito bites, and as I drove away I wondered if the answer to how to resurrect the things I lost was somehow hidden in those red, raised bites on my skin in a form of supernatural braille. In a way I was right. The answer I was looking for was already within me.

In performing the spell of the Midnight Library, I came to recognize that I carry the words in those books and the writings in those diaries within me, within my spirit, my memory, and the blood of my Ancestors rushing through my veins. I carry the stories from my childhood and my family with me as long as I am alive. The cottage, the lost journals, the ghost of the Victrola—the experience of these things gives me a strength that can never be destroyed. Not by fire, not by anything.

They belong to me. I am telling you this story because through it all, through the trials and tribulations you might face in life, through the resurrection of all that is within you that you may have forgotten or buried or thought you had lost, one of the most important things that I want to share with you in this book is:

 ## YOU ARE YOUR OWN MAGICK.

Read that again.

Nothing and no one can ever take that away from you.

Your magick is a profound life energy that is uniquely yours, and it is what I refer to as your Wild. The Wild is the pure, ancient magick within you. It is the raw, unedited force of your being, snapping you alive, vibrating with all that you have ever been, all that you are and the legacy that you will leave. It is in the stories of your Ancestors coursing through your veins, stories that your ears have never heard but that your soul knows.

There is a spell that only you can invoke, one that has made its mystical words known to you alone. That spell is the story of your life, and it is the greatest spell you will ever cast.

In this initiation I will teach you how to summon the magick of your own words, memories, and the things you hold dear to define your story and create a strong, unshakable foundation of confidence. Words are wands with which we cast our stories. It is the stories we tell ourselves that shape our lives and our beliefs about ourselves.

Be prepared to see yourself through new eyes, to journey with me into a new realm, and to find in this first initiation, without a shadow of a doubt, all the power that you hold within you.

YOUR LIFE

is

THE GREATEST

SPELL

YOU WILL

EVER CAST.

The Journey

LIKE THE HIGH PRIESTESS OF THE HIGHWAYS, you are wrapped cloaklike in a leopard-spotted blanket, curled up on the faux-leather passenger seat of my car as we cruise down a dark country highway. Muddy Waters's husky voice weaves its spell through the stereo speakers while fragrant wafts of honeysuckle drift in through the open windows. Bells hanging from the rearview mirror chime out lightly with each small bump down the dark country road. You take a breath and, leaning back, exhale deeply, cradling your head in the crook of your arm folded behind you. You let yourself be fully present in this moment: the sweet night air; the warm, soft blanket; the stars whirling overhead; the tinging bells; the ghost of Muddy Waters.

When the signal blinker click-clacks in a neat, soft rhythm, the car slows down to a near stop, then turns, tires crunching across a long, pebble driveway. A moonlit mist rolls over empty fields and behind them stands a dark, lush wood.

I kill the engine and grab a tall, thin candle and a lighter from the bag on the seat between us and ask you to wait in the car. You watch as I walk down a path of flat stone and, at the end of the walkway, crouch down to push the candle into a small mound of dirt. You see me take a nearby stick and draw a symbol in the ground, then stand tall, with my arms stretched toward the moon, chanting a rhyming incantation into the night. In one movement, my Spirit hand swings down to grip the lighter, and with the flash of the flame to the wick of the candle, a hundred-year-old cottage gently materializes out of thin air.

I catch your eye and with a wave of my hand, signal for you to join me at the cottage steps. You slowly get out of the car and walk down the path. The cottage is materializing, coming in clearer now, the weathered and delicate clapboards, the decades-old mint green paint, chipped and dull. Rusty tin cans strung together on the porch sway gently in the night breeze and make an occasional clanging sound. In the moonlight, the front of the cottage appears to lean to the right a bit, the scrollwork on its bargeboards a faded purple and the gingerbread trim a sky blue. As you approach the front porch, you can see through the antique wavy-glass windows tall candles flickering, some in old bottles, others in antique brass holders stacked upon books.

We climb the three small steps to the old porch, pass two antique rocking chairs, and continue to the mint-green wooden door. Reaching for the old brass door handle, you see that your name has been engraved into the wood and painted purple. A weathered paper tag in the shape of a skeleton key hangs from the doorknob; upon closer examination you are able to make out the words written in flowing cursive:

```
The power with which you give your name
          opens all doors for you.
```

You read it again, slowly, out loud, and as you do the wooden door creaks open on its rusty hinges.

You are drawn in by the sweet coal-fire smell of old books. Flickering cream-colored candles on the tables and windowsills illuminate handmade mahogany bookshelves lining every wall, crooked and tall like old gods holding court. In their fretwork frames, they boast books of all shapes and sizes: centuries-old clothbound tomes, edge-worn hardbacks, signed first editions, dusty leather-bound classics, and handcrafted gems with spines engraved in gold leaf. Antique handheld mirrors grace the walls. At the center of the room, three lace-embellished dresses hang above us, suspended from a line of thick twine from the highest wooden rafter. You tilt your head back to see them more clearly.

The Muses

"Those are for the Muses," I say. "They are part of a spell to coax them to come to us and whisper their knowledge to inspire our creativity and stir our imagination." I reach up to trace the fragile lace of the dress at the center. "I hung them years ago, and they've shown up in every form this place has ever taken."

"What *is* this place?" you ask.

"It is a place conjured from memory. We are standing in the ghost of my cottage that burned to the ground almost a decade ago. It is a portal that materializes with the lighting of a candle and a calling into existence. I summon it to remind me of the power that is already in me, in my memories, in the old books, in the memory of people who have inspired me, and tonight I called it into existence to help it do the same for you."

I walk toward a shelf of books and turn to face you.

"I call this place the Midnight Library, for it holds all the things within us that we often forget and need to be reminded of. You will now fill your mind and your heart with what is here and use these objects of memory to call your power back to you."

I move toward a small black cast-iron cauldron standing on three legs upon a wooden table and pull the black lighter and a pouch of frankincense and myrrh resin out of my coat pocket. On the table beside the cauldron is a pack of black charcoal disks wrapped in tinfoil, and pulling one disk out, I light it until it sparks, and then drop it delicately into the cauldron. I look at you while sprinkling yellowed pieces of resin on the hot coal in the belly of the cauldron. Hazy curls of fragrant smoke billow from the cauldron's wide mouth, the wispy white smoke slips around you like a specter, then disappears upward into the lace dresses hanging above. The smell of the resins calms you. You walk over to stand next to me at the cauldron as an antique Victrola turns itself on in the corner, spinning out a haunting, familiar melody that fills the room.

I turn to you and say, "Your memories are the lyrics of the Song of You."

I dip my forefinger into the cauldron and in a slow, circular motion, swipe my fingertip around its inner sides to gather the cooled ash.

"Within this place there is something for only you to know. You must do this alone, but before I go, I will draw a mark of magick upon you to assist in your journey. In Bohemian magick, the back of the neck is a portal for dreaming and power. It is where the Muses of inspiration can enter. In this Midnight Library, we open those portals. Are you ready?"

You nod and, turning your back to me, pull aside the strands of hair that cover the nape of your neck. I take the black cauldron ash with two fingers and paint a small crescent moon there.

"The waxing crescent moon builds toward the full moon, and it symbolizes continually growing power. The symbol of the moon is your anchor; it reminds you of what courage you have already shown in your life and of what you have already overcome. You have it all within."

In the reflection of one of the hand mirrors nailed to a nearby wall, you admire the curve of the moon in black ash. It looks powerful on the nape of your neck, your own magickal secret. You can't take your eyes off of it, and in the reflection of the mirror, I am there. You see me kiss the top of your head. When you turn around, I am gone.

Alone, you begin to look more closely about the room. You pick up a heavy magnifying dome that lies on an open atlas on a nearby table, and then, in a far corner of the library, you notice a small cherrywood desk with a crisp linen envelope sitting at the center of the desk's polished surface. Leaning over for a closer look, you find, at the center of the envelope, written in black cursive ink, your name. You pick up the envelope and break the red wax seal on the back. The typewritten letter inside reads:

What is it you want to conjure?
What is it you wish to call?

Open the wilds of your imagination like
opening a door in a wall.

The books, they are wise Oracles,
co-conspirators of your dreams,

For here in the Midnight Library, not
everything is as it seems.

The Muses make their presence known by
whispering secrets in your ears,

And on the pages of these hallowed
books, revolutionary magick appears.

Simply speak out loud what you desire,
the secret you want to manifest,

Find your Coven in the ghosts of the
books, and they will do the rest.

Taking a moment to read the rhyming incantation a few times, you then lean back against the desk and notice a golden spine on a nearby bookshelf glimmering in the candlelight. You place the letter back in the envelope and put the envelope gently back on the desk. You go back to the book and you reach for it, pulling it from the shelf. The saturated colors of the bright illustration on the cover fill you with warm feelings of nostalgia. It is one of your beloved books from childhood, and as you crack open its pages, you're overwhelmed by memories that the words and pictures, and even the feel of the pages themselves, conjure. You close your eyes and press the book against your chest. There is a feeling of magick in this discovery. Something in you is stirring; the Muses seem to be whispering.

You take the book and curl up on an oversized velvet armchair beneath the Muses' dresses. The faded book spines—soft green, yellowed ivory, sun-faded red—bulge proudly from the towering wooden shelves, as if they hold the answers to all the mysteries of humankind. The library vibrates with the presence of immortal magicians of imagination, their stories and adventures pressed into paper in black ink for eternity.

What is it you want to conjure? What is it you wish to call?

The words from the rhyming incantation roll around in your head, and as they do, from the wooden beams in the ceiling, small memories begin to float down around you like big flakes of snow, softly scattering on the floorboards, in your lap and outstretched open palms. A photo from a magazine that you had ripped out and taped to your wall. A note that made your heart swoon. A photo of you as a child, laughing. Lyrics from a song you loved, a birthday cake, the hero from a favorite story, pieces of dreams, a scrap of scrawled poetry, glimpses of trips you've taken and wild adventures printed on a page. You scramble to see them, to read them, to catch them, to hold them, rediscovering the feelings you once had and still have.

You never forgot these things, of course. They came to you so quickly. You wonder if you pushed them away, where in your mind you buried them and why, but never mind. Now they stir within you. Alive, they fall around you, then disappear.

Your memories are the lyrics of the Song of You.

You stand up and walk around the room to examine the bookshelves. Running your finger down the spines of some books and opening others, you remember the stories of adventure, love, heroism, and friendship.

Are you ready?

These are the images and colors and words that touched you, embedding possibility in your being. The books, the knowledge, the creative ideas and inspiration, the stories, the history are all a gift that stays with you. The greatest events in your life—whether accessible to your mind's eye in full or threadbare, indiscernible, even invisible—are imprinted on the library of your soul.

You have it all within.

The candles are now short stubs of burning wax around you. The books in the room start to take on the hazy specter of long-dead ghosts while the first rays of sunrise begin to stretch into the Midnight Library through the dimpled antique glass. You move toward the door as crimson, orange, and yellow rays wash the book-lined cottage. On the way, you brush your hand against the lace dresses that watched over you through the night.

"Thank you, Muses," you say. "Thank you, great oracles."

The candle flames flicker in a final dance on thin black wicks as you push open the door and step outside and forward. You don't look back; you know the Midnight Library is no longer there.

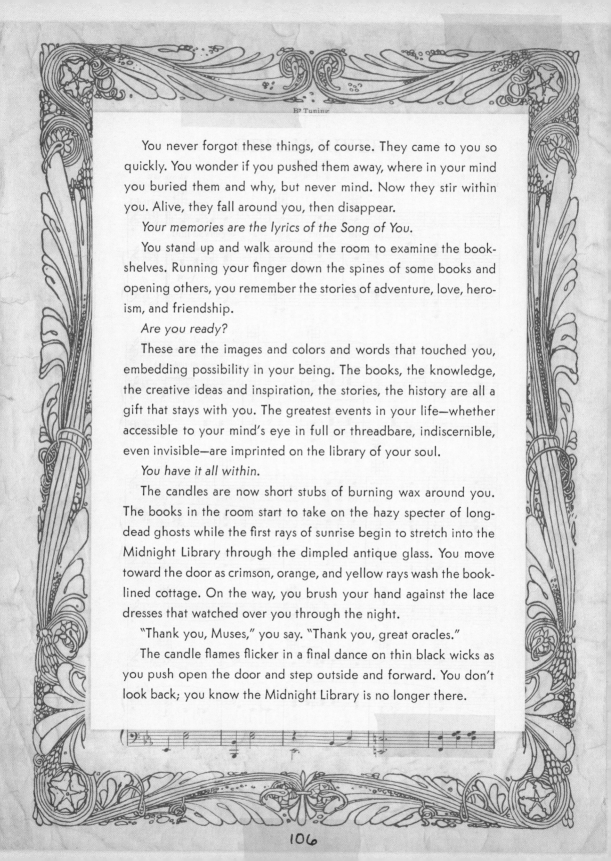

YOUR MEMORIES ARE THE LYRICS of THE SONG OF YOU.

The Spells

HELLO, I LOVE YOU

NOT ALL SPELLS REQUIRE CANDLES AND CAULDRONS. Word Witchery is my favorite way to summon powerful mojo. This simple yet profound spell is the basis for all the magick that I work, and this is why: you show others how to treat you by how you treat yourself. This includes how you speak about yourself as well as the way you speak your own name. Believe it or not, the tone in which you say your name reveals a lot about your self-esteem.

In this spell, you will learn to speak your name as a magickal word. You will speak your name clearly and powerfully, the enchanting melody of its syllables moving into the air to bewitch those around you.

You are going to let your name flow from your lips with the full belief that you are speaking the secret incantation to open the lost doors of the ancient Temple of Apollo in Delphi.

Now, you might think that this concept is simple, so simple in fact that you should just skip it and jump forward to the mind-blowing love spells.

Do not do that. If you cannot say your name as a spell, none of the spells in any book of magick will help you. They will not work because your unique power lies within you. If you cannot wield your own name with power, you will not be able to cast any spell with authority.

The way you say your name also speaks volumes about the potential power of your magick. Imagine, if you will, that you are performing a spell to call down the moon—you are reciting an invocation on a mountaintop under the stars. Do you ask the moon to be present in your sorcery in a barely audible voice, your shoulders hunched and your head down? Or do you hold your arms open to the sky, open all the power in your voice, throw your head back, and *command that moon down*? Say your name as if you are calling upon ancient gods.

109

In the Hello, I Love You spell, you will be using mirror magick to cast a deep hypnotic spell on yourself. It's been said that "the eyes are the windows to the soul," so it makes sense that when you look into your own eyes in a mirror, you can access your Wild. The key to practicing successful mirror magick is to connect with your eyes as you gaze at your reflection and then tell yourself out loud what you need to believe about yourself on the deepest level. Look deeply into your own eyes. Speaking to yourself in this way is like sending yourself a verbal love letter that you receive on a deep, subconscious level. Talking to yourself like this is a form of self-hypnotism. Weave a spell on yourself with your own words and watch the world follow suit, my darling Witch!

TOOLS AND MATERIALS

+ **A mirror in which you can see your full face**

CAST THE SPELL

1. Set the Invitation as instructed on pages 43–47.

2. In a place you will not be disturbed, sit comfortably before the mirror. Sit up straight as if there were a string at the top of your head pulling you upward. Cast your gaze upon your own eyes in the mirror. Remember that you have that power within you and that it is ready to be called upon now. Know this.

   Imagine now that you are standing in a circle with other powerful Witches on a high hill. You are wearing a long cream-colored dress that whips in the howling winds. One by one, each Witch in the circle says their name forcefully into the night sky, which responds with deep thunder and loud flashes of lightning. Now it is your turn. Look into the mirror, connect with your eyes fully, and say this phrase out loud, slowly and with strength, nine times:

   I am [full name].

3. Enchant your words. Continue to imagine standing in this circle of great and mighty Witches as you gaze into your own eyes in the mirror. You belong there with them, as none of you is frail, weak, or shy as you speak.

The words that leave your lips are spells cast with thundering power!
Now, say this phrase nine times, slowly, and with passion and intention:

> I am [full name],
> and I am someone you need to know.

4. You will feel a change happening now. It will feel like a rise in energy in
   your body. You might even get goosebumps or feel slightly lightheaded;
   that's the stirring of the Wild within. This is why mirror magick is so
   intensely profound. When you meet yourself in your own reflection and
   speak words of power, it elevates your self-esteem. Your soul hears you
   when you look into your own eyes and speak. Now, look in the mirror and
   say out loud:

> I am [full name]

Finish the rest of the sentence

> and I am someone you need to know

in your mind as if you were communicating the thought with your eyes.
Do this twenty-one times.

5. Look into the mirror and out loud this time say:

> I am [full name],
> and I stand in my full power
> to draw in the very best
> for my legendary life.
>
> See it. Be it. So be it.

Practice this spell for seven days straight to create a strong foundation from
which to build your mojo, confidence, self-love, and electrifying presence!

CROSSFIRE HURRICANE

FTER INQUIRING ABOUT YOUR NAME, THE second question people most often ask is the hopelessly boring "Where are you from?"

Consider these two answers:

Basic option: "I grew up in Florida."

Mojo option: "I grew up in the slow heat of the swampland and the mangrove trees on the river. I am the firstborn daughter to five generations of firstborn women. I was born in a sultry springtime heatwave under the sign of Taurus, ruled by Venus. I arrived marked with a kiss of fire on my right wrist that I still carry to this day."

Who would you rather meet?

When Keith Richards wrote "I was born in a crossfire hurricane," the first line of "Jumpin' Jack Flash," he was talking about himself. He was born during World War II to the sounds of sirens and blasts of air raids and bombs. The song is its own thing, of course—it's not biographical, but it was born of a literal bang that begat a colorful, crazy life story: "howled at my ma in the driving rain," "raised by a toothless, bearded hag," "crowned with a spike right through my head." And the way Mick Jagger belts it out is ferocious, the lyrics are precise and powerful, and the energy of Jack's persona is inspiring.

> ## Do not live in a story that
> ## is too small for you.

Dare to paint yourself among gods and ancient lore. Blasphemy? Maybe. But isn't it more blasphemous not to grab this life with both hands and squeeze the sweet, succulent juice out of every second until your dying breath?

The Crossfire Hurricane spell will help you see yourself and your life story anew. It will empower you to paint your life story with poetry, not unlike a great rock poet whose lyrics create an iconic song. We love to sing along to those lyrics because they are swirling with power and art and legend. They are what we wish we could be—and we can be! Your life is your art. This spell gives deep respect to the power of your life story. When you allow yourself to see yourself as legendary, you can become legendary. Rise up and claim your magick of you! Bewitch yourself in your own story.

TOOLS AND MATERIALS

- ✦ Grimoire or journal
- ✦ Pen
- ✦ One sheet of 8½ × 11-inch parchment paper
- ✦ Tape
- ✦ Twine or ribbon
- ✦ Mirror, any size

CAST THE SPELL

1. Set the Invitation as instructed on pages 43–47.

2. Write down the answers to the following questions in your personal grimoire or journal.

What phase was the moon in?

What was the weather like?

What were the surroundings of the land near where you were born? Rivers, mountains, deserts, valleys, forests?

What wildlife, birds, plants, and trees are native to the place you were born?

What astrological sign were you born under? What element is it—air, fire, earth, or water? What planet rules that sign?

What time were you born?

You can also look up your birthdate to see what historical events, discoveries, and so on occurred that day.

3. Summon your legendary mojo. This is a vital step, so don't skip over it. Close your eyes and imagine yourself as the hero of a story. Sometimes that can be hard, so let's just take a page from some wild Hollywood blockbuster film and imagine yourself as the star of the film. It's the last scene. You've saved the day—and you are done! You're walking with a swagger in slow motion as everything blows up behind you and you turn around and light your cigarette off the wreckage as the music kicks in. Conjure that kind of hero vibe.

4. Then take the piece of parchment paper and write at the top, **I am [full name]**. Underneath that, write down three of your favorite responses to the questions you answered in step 2.

5. Tape this piece of paper to a mirror for nine days. Every time you look in the mirror, read these sentences aloud and look at your reflection as you do. This is a mirror magick technique of sticking words to your image—and it works.

6. After nine days, roll the parchment into a scroll toward you to bring those words into you. Tie the scroll with twine or ribbon. Hang it over the door on the inside of your bedroom or above your bed. As we continue our hot spellworking journey, you will be using these sentences you wrote to enhance other spells, and later we will be using these words to make a powerful amulet for you.

IF YOU WANT TO ACHIEVE GREATNESS STOP ASKING FOR PERMISSION

WALK THIS WAY

THE WORDS THAT WE USE TO DESCRIBE ourselves are the cloaks of our own design. We wrap our stories and our experiences around us just like clothing. Don't believe me? Watch any film, television show, or music video with the sound off, and I guarantee that you will know who has the mojo just by how they walk and move.

Our self-confidence and our capacity for self-love are directly tied into the words we use to either honor or destroy ourselves. When you attach positive, powerful, and sensual words to your self-description, it is an act of self-love and an honoring of your Wild.

The Walk This Way spell is designed to amplify your own power and confidence by using positive descriptive words that you "attach" to your aura. Imagine going to a perfume counter, spraying an intoxicating scent into the air, and walking through the cloud of it. The fragrance clings to you. This spell is exactly like that, but rather than fragrance, bold descriptive words illuminate the essence of what you want to be out in the world.

When you do this spell, it is important to dress the part. Research has shown that dressing with intention and confidence boosts our self-esteem and our mood. It not only communicates to others a nonverbal message about how we feel about ourselves but also reflects back on our own confidence and self-esteem when we look in the mirror.

How do you want to feel? What is the clothing or makeup that you dig the most that gives you power? Sid Vicious had his chain and metal lock necklace, Billie Holiday had her white gardenias, and John Lennon had his round, wire-rimmed glasses. Use your adornments like magickal tools for this spell.

I like to do this spell every year, either on my birthday or New Year's Eve because it is not only a powerful spell, but it is also a great way to check in with yourself on a yearly basis! This spell helps define who you want to be and sets you on the course to achieve it. Let's get your mojo rising, sweet Witch!

Passionate.
Unstoppable.
Magnetic.

Mandy

Powerful.
Radiant.
Sensual.

Queen.

TOOLS AND MATERIALS

- ✦ Your personal grimoire or a journal
- ✦ Nine 8-inch white taper candles
- ✦ Carving tool (any clay carving tool, pencil, or small pocketknife)
- ✦ Matches
- ✦ Nonflammable surface on which to burn the candles such as a medium-sized terracotta clay saucer that comes with a planter (you can buy the saucers separately) or a china plate

CAST THE SPELL

1. Set the Invitation as instructed on pages 43–47.

2. Imagine for a moment that you are going to be on the cover of a top magazine with twenty million subscribers. You happen to know one of the writers, who owes you a favor. You will be able to choose nine words that they will print next to your cover photograph to describe you.

3. In your personal grimoire, write down as many adjectives as you like to describe this empowered version of yourself. Even if you don't feel aligned with bold descriptions of yourself right now, consider that whatever words are put on this magazine cover, twenty million people around the world are going to see them and believe them. Allow yourself to blow your own mind.

4. Narrow your list down to the nine adjectives that feel the most electric, bold, and badass to you. You can even say them out loud and see how they sound together!

5. Beginning at the top of the candle and working downward, use your carving tool to inscribe one adjective on each candle.

6. Once you've inscribed a word on every candle, light one and drip a small pool of wax on the terracotta saucer or china plate. Press the bottom of the lit candle into the wet wax; hold the candle upright until the wax hardens enough to keep the lit candle in place.

7. Light the second candle from the wick of the first, again dripping a small pool of wax on the saucer or plate and letting it harden so that the candle will remain in place. When it is set, light the third candle from its wick. Repeat until all nine candles are lit. As you light each candle, say:

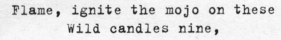

```
My name is [full name] and I am
      [word on that candle].
```

8. Once you have lit all the candles, repeat this invocation three times:

```
Flame, ignite the mojo on these
        Wild candles nine,

    I hereby will the words and
       my being to entwine.

    For every day that passes,
     my confidence does surge,

  By the nine enchanted candles,
      carved with my own words.
```

After you repeat the invocation three times, close with:

```
        See it. Be it. So be it.
```

9. Look at the candle flames and imagine the words attaching themselves to your being. When you feel them in your bones, blow out the candles and watch the smoke trail into the sky.

Sit in front of the candles and repeat steps 6 to 8 of the ritual every day for nine days. At the end of day nine, burn the candles down completely to seal the spell. Wrap the remaining candle wax in a cloth or put in a resealable bag and place under your mattress so you can sleep and dream while soaking up all those powerful vibes!

MAGIC BUS

THE MAGIC BUS SPELL SUMMONS A POWERFUL group of your heroes from the Afterlife to assist you in manifesting your desires. Think of this spell as an opportunity to form your very own supernatural board of directors—all invested in helping you achieve your dreams. Imagine hanging out with heroes who no longer walk the earth as they share their mojo, expertise, and wisdom with you.

In this spell, your destination is your dream, babe, and you've got a ticket to ride! Now imagine that you have six companions hanging out with you on this psychedelic bus, people who inspire you and whose advice you'd seek if you could readily consult them, since they have been down the road you wish to travel. They know the shortcuts, the places to avoid, and the best ways to go. They are here to help you have the trip of your life and get to your dream destination in style.

The spell focuses on a single aspiration and a group of six people you've chosen to help you. It uses visual magick that enables you to see yourself surrounded by support!

When you are calling upon the Spirits, it is a tradition in the magick of Bohemia to make an offering. Generally, these offerings are vices, treats, or sweet things—perhaps alcohol or cigarettes, chocolate, or flowers. If you can find things that the person loved in life, it will help your cause. As an example, I might offer a flower crown for Frida Kahlo, a pack of Turkish cigarettes for Leonard Cohen, or a psychedelic silk neck scarf for Jimi Hendrix.

Before you begin, write down and answer this question in your grimoire:

> What is one thing that I wish to be or one goal that I want to achieve in my life
>
> that I could use some supernatural help or guidance with?

Below your answer, write down the following question:

> Who are six people in the Afterlife who inspire me and who embody a trait that I wish to possess or have successfully done what I want to do?

Choose six people in the Afterlife you admire or who inspire you and who have successfully done what you want to do while they were alive. Once you've decided and gathered your tools, proceed to step 1 of the preparation.

TOOLS AND MATERIALS

+ Images of the six supernatural superstars who you've chosen to accompany you on your journey, photocopied in color and cut to 4 × 6 inches or printed out in color to the same size on either luster or matte photo paper. It can be a mix of vertical and horizontal images.

+ Your favorite photograph of yourself, also photocopied or printed in color and cut to 4 × 6 inches

+ Glue stick
+ Seven 4 × 6 inch note cards
+ One pair multipurpose scissors
+ Seven tealight candles
+ Matches
+ Offerings for the Spirits (see page 127)

1. Use a glue stick to mount a note card to the back of each photo to make it stiff enough to lean against something and remain upright. Use the scissors to trim around the edges so that all the cards are the same size if necessary.

2. Clear a special space to set up your supernatural board of directors. The images must stand upright, so use a single shelf or a small table pushed against the wall.

3. Assemble your gang in your chosen location. Stand your picture at center, and place three heroes to each side of you. This is important visual magick, as it allows you to see yourself surrounded by support. Step back and admire your badass gang of inspiration.

CAST THE SPELL

1. Place a tealight candle in front of each photo. Strike a match once and light the first wick, then amplify the power of the flame by lighting each candle from the previous one. With each flame that you light and place in front of a photo, say:

```
I call upon you, [their full name], to
        help guide me on my way.
      I give you this offering
 in thanks for your inspiration and
              guidance.
```

Then add your own personal words of what you'd like to say to them. In my experience with connecting with the Spirit realm, I have found that it is helpful to talk to them out loud, as if they are sitting there with you. Go for it! Let it out. Don't censor your conversations; tell them anything that is in your heart.

2. Set up the offerings to the Spirits in front of their individual photos and candles.

3. Now, standing before your gang, recite this invocation three times:

```
I summon Muses and Spirits, heroic and wise,

   Help to guide my truest vision and be
                my allies.

 Give me the courage to do the thing that
                I dream,

Brave and inspired by this supernatural team.
```

To cast the spell in motion, say:

See it. Be it. So be it.

4. Take the time to work on your dream while the tealights are burning. Blow out the candles when you are finished, then thank and say goodbye to your supernatural friends. You can relight or replace candles to keep this badass gang of inspiration altar going whenever you are working on your dream. It will help to keep you motivated and in good company. The constant visual reminder helps activate the magick on a deeper level and it brings strong results!

NOTE: Leave the offerings at your altar for as long as it's appropriate for your spell; freshen them up when needed. When you feel like you have received the motivation and mojo needed from your gang or your current project is drawing to a close, you can bury the offerings in the ground or bring them to a cemetery and leave them just inside the gates. Take the photos and tape them into your grimoire so you can always have the support of your supernatural gang.

INITIATION II

WE CAN BE HEROES

ROWING UP, MOST OF US WERE FED FAERIE TALES
of heroes rushing in to save the day.

Witches don't wait for anyone to save us.

We save ourselves.

The courage to heal is an act of bravery. Prepare to call your power back to you and unleash the warrior Witch within as you deepen your sense of self-protection, strength, and capable confidence in this initiation. The following fierce spells are heroic calls to action that will change your outlook on life and will put the power back in your hands. Once you've completed them, the results will adorn you like phantom medals of honor.

The spells in this initiation will help you:

+ **destroy obstacles that keep you from your truest self**
+ **learn how to shield and protect yourself from bad vibes**
+ **heal a rift, soothe misunderstandings, or gain closure with compassion**

I will guide you through rare and unusual rituals that you won't find anywhere else. They work because they are action-driven, physical ways to heal that speak to a primal need in our souls. We'll be burning switchblade-carved candles upside down, swinging a hammer to shatter poisoned plates, looking upon sanitation workers as angels, and using hot-pink wax drippings to heal personal rifts supernaturally. If you give yourself over to the process, you will gain a greater sense of personal strength and confidence with each spell that you cast. The time has come to work your own Wild sorcery to let the Witch in you rise!

The Journey

THE NIGHT FOREST AWAITS YOU. YOU STAND before a path of deep green moss lined on either side with phosphorescent mushrooms of various sizes and shapes glowing a brilliant orange. The full moon's spectral luster hovers over the high curving tree branches, which, like great long-reaching arms, create an enchanted canopy above the path. Crickets fill the sultry air with their evening song as does the sweet, sharp scent of pine. You move forward slowly, taking in the magick of this strange place, your feet sinking into the soft moss. All around, fireflies flash occasionally through the trees in the dark.

You walk for a short while in the dark silence. Then, up ahead, you see a different sort of flickering: the flames of tall cream-colored candles perched in a cluster of chandeliers suspended from branches of the canopy and swaying slightly in the faint, warm breeze. You follow the light to the end of the path, which narrows to its close at a towering, ornate wrought-iron gate. A short distance beyond the closed gate, you see what appears to be a clearing of some sort, with a long banquet table with chairs positioned at the other side, and one at its head.

You reach for the latch, and the gate creaks open to a high meadow where the table sits a minute's walk in, beckoning you. You take a few careful steps forward into the meadow, and, as you do, you look around: you're alone.

Upon reaching one end of the long table, you find it set elaborately for what appears to be a ghostly feast: white bone china, silver, and lace adorn its weathered wood surface. Dozens of dripping wax candles line its center from end to end, illuminating it with a warm glow. There are thirteen mismatched high-back chairs—six on each side and one at the far end.

Not far beyond the table, farther into the clearing, you notice a large tree stump. There are symbols carved into its bark. A silver hammer is laid out on the stump's flat surface. Broken pieces of shattered porcelain are scattered about, both on the stump and the surrounding grass. This appears to be some sort of ceremonial place. You suddenly feel nervous, a strange tightening in your throat, and decide to leave. You look for the gate and the path out of the clearing, but all you see is dark forest. You are able to focus only on the great table, which draws you to it. There, the glow from the candle flames reveal words written boldly in black marker upon the plates. You approach the plate closest to you and read it:

```
     I feel completely misunderstood and
            alone in this world.
```

You freeze. You know that feeling. Seeing it written down in words, though, hits hard. You slowly move down that side of the table to read the other five plates.

```
I feel like no one has ever truly loved me.
       I'm worried that I don't fit in.
      Everyone is better than I am.
      I've been a failure at everything.
            I hate my body.
```

You take a deep breath and cross to the table's other side to read the other six:

```
I'm not smart enough, no matter how hard I try.
I deserve all the bad things that happen to me.
          I feel like a fraud.
      It's too late; I missed my chance.
```

You pause over the last plate at the head of the table, looking up when you hear the bumpy scratch of wood being dragged on dirt. The chair at the head of the table has been pulled out for you to sit down. The plate before it is empty, a black marker sitting next to it with the silverware.

Welcome to the Feast of Poisoned Words, where the plates hold the destructive thoughts that we feed ourselves.

Language can be lethal. What poison words have you fed yourself in your life? What poisons have you allowed yourself to consume from the words of others, from society, from familiar unloving voices within you? This ritual is the exorcism of an evil you've allowed to live inside you—a powerful evil that requires a powerful ritual to cast it out.

You grab the marker and write a sentence, then another, and another. The wounded words, the angry words, the devastating words, pour out of your soul onto the plate.

A sudden wind blows the candle flames to dance and then disappear into trailing puffs of smoke like ghosts. In the darkness, you hear the rattle and crash of porcelain shattering over and over; then the night falls silent again. The candle before your place setting slowly flickers alive on its own. The entire banquet table has been cleared. The only two objects that remain on the great, long table are your plate covered in poisonous words and a single candle. Out of the darkness, dozens of fireflies appear, circling the ceremonial stump, illuminating it, the shards of porcelain, and the silver hammer.

You now understand: you can either continue to feed yourself the poison words on the table every day or you can choose to name them, smash them into bits, and bury their remains. My darling Witch, prepare to grab your hammer.

The Spells

SEARCH and DESTROY

THE NEGATIVE WORDS THAT YOU TELL YOURSELF are hexes you impose on your own life. Whether the words recall a past version of yourself that you've outgrown, or they are someone else's words that you've allowed to haunt you, if you let your heart believe them, you give your power away. Identifying and removing those words from your mind may be the biggest battle that you will wage in your lifetime, because the enemy is within—and it feeds on your fear.

Grandma Helen used to say that FEAR stands for Forgetting Everything is All Right. She believed that fear is an emotion that comes up to hold us back from doing phenomenal things. I'm willing to bet that most things that you are proud of achieving in your life started with a deep feeling of fear that you bravely ignored or conquered. In that sense, fear may be a powerful clue to something you want to do or express. On the other side of the door of fear is the extraordinary life you were meant to lead. Take my hand and let's push through it together.

In this spell, I will guide you through calling your power back to you in the same way, by banishing words that wish to destroy you. And part of the thrill, my dear Witch, is the way in which we are going to do that!

This ritual works because it ignites something deeply instinctive. It allows us to release hurt and anger freely, with absolute force and without a hint of inhibition, in a way that most of us have never had permission to do in our lives.

Some of the most exhilarating personal transformations that I've ever seen took place at my Witch Camp, where we go out to the tree-stump altar in a field surrounded by forest to carry out this ritual. We perform it on our first night gathering because under the cloak of night there is greater freedom for full expression. In the darkness, it is easier to confess the things that we allow to hold us back. It is easier to cry, to scream, to let our faces screw up in agony.

The ceremony begins as we gather in a circle around the tree-stump altar. Each person holds a single lit candle, and we stand silently in our illuminated circle for a moment. When I tell them what we are about to do, their faces change. They are apprehensive, surprised, even terrified.

I go first. I step into the center of the circle and read the poisonous words I've written on my plate out loud into the night like curses, then I swing the hammer back over my shoulder and let out a guttural scream as it crashes down to shatter the porcelain plate.

At first, I feel their shock and their silence: *Am I allowed to do this?* We are taught to fix things, to soothe and to smooth everything over, not to break things violently. Yet when we take that physical action against our own demons, it heals us on a deep level. I have seen the transformation as one by one they smash their own plates to bits and walk away from the stump triumphant, the hammer raised above their heads as they howl to the night sky in victory.

Take your power back! Protect yourself! Fight! Too many times in life, we've been told to be nice, sit down, and be quiet. We stifle our feelings; we repress who we truly are. You can find your strength in the feelings or parts of yourself that society doesn't want you to express, and you can transform it into your own raw power. So, let it all go and obliterate the stories you tell yourself, the hurt, and the anger. This spell is your liberation. This spell is your resurrection. Be brave, dear Witch, and bring the hammer down!

TOOLS AND MATERIALS

+ **One 12-inch white dinner plate**
+ **Black marker**
+ **Standard pillow cover with zipper**
+ **Two heavy-duty eight-gallon (kitchen sized) garbage bags**
+ **Safety goggles or other eye protection**
+ **Hammer**

CAST THE SPELL

1. Set the Invitation as instructed on pages 43–47.

2. With the black marker, write down all the things that have made you feel unlovable and unworthy. Don't censor yourself. These words are your wounds. Write down all the things you currently shame, scold, or terrorize yourself with. Write down the demoralizing things you tell yourself about yourself—the kinds of things that if you heard someone else say to your five-year-old self, you just might consider calling the authorities. Remember: the more raw and real the words are, the more exhilarating they will be to smash!

3. Read aloud the words you wrote. Doing so is an act of calling out the things you want to destroy. When you give them attention *on your own terms,* you call your power back to you, which means they won't have the dark hold on you that they once did.

   If you do this spell with a friend, sharing the words out loud is often very helpful in taking back your power, as we all fight similar demons. Even just the realization of that fact helps dissipate the influence of the poisonous words.

is under
STOOD
Eve
chance.
I missed
Cham
ERYTHING
PAST
SCAPE
PAIN.

4. It's time to destroy your demons! Put the plate in a garbage bag, then put it into the pillow cover. Zip up the pillow cover and put it inside the second trash bag and tie it securely.

5. Take your safety goggles, hammer, and the wrapped-up plate somewhere outside to destroy it safely. If you live in the city, you can do this on the roof of your building, in an alley, or at a playground or park when there's no one around.

6. Put on your safety goggles. Place the bag on a hard surface, like a tree stump, a big flat stone, or concrete. Grab that hammer and destroy that plate! Feel the powerful pleasure of breaking apart the things that would have destroyed you.

7. Throw your head back and howl! Feel the exhilaration of the Wild jolting through your being. Nothing can stop you.

8. Now, let's bury the dead. There are two important things you must do that are essential to the success of this spell. First, throw the bag in a trash can with a lid that is *outside* your home. Second, once you put the lid on the can, turn your back, walk away, and *don't look back*.

REMEMBER: sanitation workers can be angels. When I've done this spell at home in the city, I've made sure to wake up at 6:00 A.M., when the garbage truck arrives, to take my poisoned words away. I stick my head out of my fourth-floor window and cackle as their compactor smashes the pieces even more. Then I watch in glee as they disappear from my street to bring it to the dump where it all belongs.

DON'T LIVE

A STORY

THAT IS

TOO SMALL

FOR YOU.

RETURN to SENDER

THERE ARE MANY REASONS YOU'D RETURN AN unopened letter to its sender, but imagine you know that the contents of the letter is toxic. You don't want to engage with the low realms of hate and negativity, so you simply deflect it by sending it right back. Similarly, this old Bohemian spell helps protect you from bad vibes by returning them, as you might return a letter, to the person who generated them.

This is *the* spell to do if someone is gossiping about you, messing with you, trying to break up your relationship, or throwing bad mojo your way.

For the Return to Sender spell to be successful, it is important to focus simply on reflecting the energy sent your way back to its source and nothing more. The spell is a shield, bouncing the bad vibes back and, in the process, releasing their harmful intentions from you. It's also vital that you do not add your anger, hatred, fear, or loss to the spell. If you do, it won't work. You don't have time to waste on toxic people because doing so just feeds their power. Performed as instructed, this spell puts all the power back into your own hands, where it belongs.

TOOLS AND MATERIALS

- ✦ One 5-inch candle
- ✦ Carving tool (any clay carving tool, pencil, or small pocketknife)
- ✦ Wood cutting board
- ✦ Utility knife
- ✦ Lighter
- ✦ Candleholder

146

CAST THE SPELL

1. Set the Invitation as instructed on pages 43–47.

2. With the carving tool, carve the words "Return to Sender" into the candle. Begin about one half inch from the top, where the wick is, and carve so that the phrase reads vertically down the side of the candle.

3. Lay the candle on a cutting board. With your utility knife, slice off about one half inch of the candle on the wick end—without cutting into "Return"—so that the candle is flat on both top and bottom and no wick shows.

4. Flip the candle upside down so that the original bottom of the candle is facing up. "Return to Sender" will read upside down and the letters will be facing in the wrong direction.

5. Place the candle upside down in a candleholder. By burning the candle in this position, you will send the energy back to whomever sent it to you.

6. With a lighter, hold a continuous flame over the new top of the candle for about sixty seconds. The wax will melt and reveal the wick.

7. Begone! Burn the candle in a safe place. As it burns down, the candle will release all the negative thoughts, bad vibes, and drama that aren't yours. Allow the candle to completely burn down in one sitting, occasionally glancing at it to take pleasure in the fact that it is disappearing more from your life, but don't meditate over it. It's not your business what other people think about you. You're just sending back what isn't yours.

8. Once the candle has burned down, scrape off any remaining wax from the candleholder. Dispose of the wax away from your home, either by burying it in the ground or tossing it in an outdoor trash can. Once you have disposed of the wax, leave the site and do not look back. Know that every forward step you take is one step further away from the drama.

BREAK on THROUGH to the OTHER SIDE

MISTAKES HAVE BEEN MADE, FEELINGS HAVE been hurt, mournful songs of regret have been playing on repeat. This Bohemian candle spell works as supernatural surgery to heal a rift while sending healing energy, understanding, and compassion to all involved. Performing it before trying to make amends with the person involved will help the talks exponentially. Of course, all people have free will and not all hurts can be mended, but at the very least you will heal the hurt in yourself by performing it.

TOOLS AND MATERIALS

- One 9-inch white taper candle
- Carving tool (any clay carving tool, pencil, or small pocketknife)
- Wood cutting board
- Tinfoil or parchment paper
- One pink chime or taper candle
- Lighter
- Photo of the person you want to heal a rift with
- Candleholder
- Standard size or small envelope

CAST THE SPELL

1. Set the Invitation as explained on pages 43–47.

2. Break the white candle in half, but don't separate the halves; allow the wick to remain. The wick symbolizes the energetic cord between you and the other person, and the broken wax symbolizes the rift itself.

3. With your carving tool, inscribe your name on one of the two broken pieces. Repeat for the other person on the remaining half of the candle.

4. Cover the cutting board with a layer of tinfoil or parchment paper.

5. Take the candle and hold it by its wick to slide the two broken pieces together again. Lay the candle on its side.

6. Light the pink candle and drip its wax into the crack of the broken white candle. As you drip the pink wax to heal the break, whisper this invocation repeatedly:

Wax to heal, fire to feel, love to seal.

7. The hot wax from the pink candle will start to repair the broken white candle. Slowly rotate it and allow the pink wax to fill in the break all the way around the candle.

8. Once the break is completely filled with pink wax, stop chanting. Let the wax cool and set for ten minutes on the tinfoil- or parchment-covered cutting board.

9. Look at the person's photograph. Imagine the best possibilities and outcomes for healing to take place. Imagine meeting up with this person and that they are open to healing this rift too. See a conversation between the two of you that is kind and generates understanding and genuine apology. End the visualization by giving them a hug or waving goodbye.

10. Once the pink wax has cooled, set the fully repaired candle of white and pink wax into a candleholder. Light the candle. Repeat three times:

Flame alight, set it right.

11. The spell is cast. Sit with the candle as it burns for the first half hour, visualizing a radiant pink healing light filling your chest and beaming outward toward the person you are performing it for. Keeping an eye on the candle, let it burn down completely. The healing has begun.

Initiation III

A SELF·LOVE SUPREME

IMAGINE YOU'RE DRIVING DOWN A LONG STRETCH of dark, narrow highway in the middle of nowhere. It's just you and the broken yellow lines of the road in the glow of your headlights. You see nothing for miles, then you take a deep bend in the road and see a neon sign, bright, flashing. As you get closer, you can see that its tubes are bent in curves swirling with vibrating light.

You reach the sign and get out of the car. The voltage of current is amped up, traveling with intensity in one direction, then dropping off as a second line picks up and drives the energy back up high again. The light hums and sizzles, pops and cracks. Over and over again, the process repeats. Electric vein, electric artery: life blood in the glass tubes that spell your name.

This is what I imagine self-love to be, and I call it the Electric.

The Electric is a core belief in your own power, presence, and truth. It is essential to your life force and well-being. It charges your life and your spells with greater focus, determination, and willpower. The Electric is the unshakable belief— your arms held to the sky, your head back, your voice howling, that you can wield your Wild and you are, in fact, capable of anything.

In a world that tries to make us feel that we are lacking in some way, self-love is a revolutionary act. I was in my mid-twenties when I had

my first glimpse of women of all ages, backgrounds, and body types celebrating themselves.

I had gone to a burlesque show at the Slipper Room in New York City with a friend. That evening, the red velvet curtains opened onto a dark stage, empty except for a tall pillar candle in a glass cylinder. The flame flickered for a few minutes, then a Rubenesque blonde—covered in about thirty pink balloons from front to back, from her neck to the middle of her thigh, her feet shod in hot-pink stilettoes dotted with crystals and wielding a long cigarette holder in one hand—appeared onstage. She sauntered over to the candle, hips swaying, and dipped the end of her cigarette holder purposefully into the candle flame. She took a deep drag, slowly scanned the audience with her sultry eyes, and then proceeded to pop the pink balloons off her body with the lit end in time to the beat of some old burlesque music. She smiled mischievously as each balloon exploded under the burning hot tip of her cigarette, exposing more of her skin with each loud bang. By the time she was nearly naked, in all her full-figured, curvy glory, she had successfully mesmerized me: Her energy was electrifying, sensual, and smoldering, and it filled the room. She carried herself with a radiant confidence that enveloped the audience with something that felt like joy or love or both.

I turned to the friend who was with me that night and said, "You know what she has that I don't? Self-love."

The performer's name was Dirty Martini, and she kept a spell on that crowd after she was offstage and gliding over to the bar in a pink G-string, with a fluffy baby pink feather boa sliding demurely off her naked shoulders. Every ounce of my body wanted what she had. I wanted to carry myself like a queen and hold my head high like her. Watching her confidence in action gave me what was then a rare example in my life of a woman owning her power.

It takes a lot of work to love yourself. First, you must accept that loving yourself is not an act of egotism, but an embracing of who you truly are without outside influence. Loving yourself is also the ultimate rebellion in a society that determines what is acceptable, normal, and beautiful. More often than not, socially crafted standards affect our self-esteem, making us feel like we are less than we truly are and fueling endless

152

competition among ourselves about what is the best way of thinking, doing, and being. When we can fully acknowledge this deep flaw in our society, and when we choose not to participate in this destructive way of thinking, that is when we call our true power back to us.

Part of the allure of being a Witch is identifying with who we are and not falling in line with a prescribed notion of what we are expected to do and who we are supposed to be. At Witch Camp, we have genuine conversations as we craft our magick. These talks help spur change and growth; they help us take our power back from those who wish to keep us feeling small.

I remember one Witch Camp when there were twenty of us, all women, sitting together in a circle in a field.

"I realized that when I don't love myself, I see other women as enemies," said one Witch.

Nineteen other heads nodded in the soft glow of the moon coming through the trees.

She continued, "I don't want to be that person anymore. I've never been around a group of women this compassionate and caring. I've only known competition. I've watched all of you root each other on and care about each other's lives and progress, and I felt myself being a part of that. I felt it being real."

"A rising tide lifts all the boats," another voice chimed in. "It's true. When we feel good about ourselves, we can take that good feeling and share it with others, and its effect multiplies."

Another Witch said, "That idea of a rising tide lifting all the boats helps me the most when I'm not feeling good. If I can focus my

153

energy on helping someone else in need, not only do they end up feeling better and supported, but that good feeling also boomerangs back on me and lifts me up."

The next day would be our last full day together, and we were preparing to take our vows of self-love marriage in the river. We sat in the circle, writing our vows and sharing them with each other. Before each of us sat an unlit candle into which we'd carefully etched personally meaningful symbols, anointed with sweet-smelling oils, and adorned with glitter. We blew good wishes on our own candles to begin the process of giving them life, then we passed them around the full circle for each Witch to blow life and support onto them. We arranged the candles in a circle on a bed of rocks, then lit them from a single flame to strengthen the power of the vows we would make to ourselves in the morning. Reading our vows out loud is always a part of the evening's ritual.

In the particular year that I'm describing, a magickal thing happened. In the weeks before we gathered for camp, I put out a public request asking people if they would like to write a vow of self-love for the Witches of Witch Camp to read out loud on that last evening. I received four hundred replies from all over the world! So, on this last night, after everyone in the circle read their own vows, we each read another twenty from those that were sent in. With every vow we read, the energy of our group grew. As the vows were voiced by candlelight, our small group of twenty transformed to the energy of four hundred Witches standing strong together!

The spells in this Initiation are designed to boost self-confidence, increase a sense of well-being, and help you embrace the bewitching beauty that is yours alone. With my good wishes and those of your Witch Camp sisters and brothers who have performed these rituals, I pass them on to you. Stand with your arms raised beneath a glorious full moon and call its supreme enchantment down to imbue you with self-love and power. Discover and learn how to tap into your own secret self-compass in order to resolve important life questions without compromising who you are. Reconnect with the child within you to awaken self-compassion. Prepare to fall madly in love with yourself as you write self-love vows and perform a ritual ceremony. An invitation to your Electric awaits.

SAYING YES

TO YOUR MAGICK

IS A

REVOLUTIONARY ACT.

The Journey

THE ENVELOPE UNDER YOUR DOOR IS ADORNED with golden glitter and redolent with an alluring peppermint. Inside, a message written in a calligraphic hand reads:

The Rising Tide Shall Lift Your Boat,

But Only a True Vow Makes It Float.

Enter the Wood at the Stump of the Ancient Pine,

Follow the Light to What Is Yours and Mine.

TOMORROW, 11:11 P.M.

The Journey Is Yours Alone.

At the appointed time, you enter a wood of tall pine trees. The trees are all the same but covered in various degrees of moss and lichen and growing in a formation so tight you wonder if you will ever find the way to the river and back. Short, jagged, leafless branches line their trunks in irregular intervals like giant broken combs. The wood buzzes with the low drone of crickets trilling an incessant serenade in a world that is seemingly black.

The note said to look to the light as a guide, so you take a few steps, instantly comforted by the moonlight sifting through the tangle of pine branches, beaming down here and there, here and there, as you move forward slowly, searching for a light. The ancient woods slope downward, and as you walk you see a spark—at least you think you do. It fades out but comes back, fades out but comes back, fades out but comes back. You move hesitantly yet quickly over moss and toward the light: a small hurricane lantern with a handle on a twisted stump, a vibrant red candle carved with a large radiant sun and decorated with golden glitter burning within. It smells like peppermint. You pick up the lantern to light your way on what appears to be a dirt path just a few feet away.

As you come through the trees, you find a small wooden canoe bobbing lightly on the moonlit water, tied with a long rope to a gnarled tree trunk on the bank. Its outside lengths are decorated with beautiful hand-carved spirals, stars, and magickal symbols. A worn metal lantern just like the one you hold is suspended from a black wrought-iron hook affixed to a post on the bow. Within the lantern burns a red candle with a curving heart etched into it. On the back of the candle are letters that spell your name.

Your very own Abracadabra.

It all belongs to you.

You feel a rush of energy as you place the lantern with the red candle on the belly of the canoe. You step into the boat, balancing yourself as the water rocks it slightly from side to side. You sit down, pick up the paddle, and begin to move through the water, a bit awkwardly at first, in the direction of another glowing lantern with a red candle down the river on the opposite bank. As you paddle closer to where the lantern sits, you see something moving on the water. You paddle closer and discover a lone cream-colored folded paper boat bobbing on the tide. You pick it up, and by the light of your lantern, you can see there is writing on the inside. You unfold the boat and read the words aloud and then the name of the person who wrote them:

```
I vow to love myself unconditionally and
always remember the Electric that exists
   within me to bring magick to my days.
             —SILVANA
```

You fold the curved paper back into the shape of the boat, then set it back in the water. Up ahead, the river curves and grows wider, revealing more tall, carved candles burning along the riverbank and a fleet of cream-colored tiny paper boats bobbing in the steady current, their vows waiting to be read:

```
I vow to honor, love, and nurture the child
        self in me. —DYLAN MONROE
```

```
I vow to be kind to myself and treat myself
       with respect and love. —SUSIE LEE
```

```
I vow to never take my life for granted.
I vow to see the beauty all around me always.
             —ELIZABETH
```

I vow to treat my body, my heart, and my soul
like the temples that they are. —SAGE

I vow to continue to heal, grow, evolve,
and learn.

I vow to support my evolution and cheer myself
on in every step of the journey. —SHANA

As you pick up each paper boat, speaking its vow and the name of the person who wrote it, you send that good wish and support back out into the world toward them like a sweet spell into the night. It feels good. Your handling of the canoe becomes easier with each message you read; your paddling becomes smoother, stronger, and more purposeful, fueled by an almost electric energy vibrating within your body. These words are working their own magick on you, too. As you come around another bend in the river, a small, weathered dock dotted with more candlelit lanterns comes into view. You're paddling toward the dock when, at the river's edge to your left, you see a little paper boat capsize, then get stuck in a bed of rocks where the river runs shallow near the bank. You move toward the boat, but as you do, your paddle digs into the sand; you don't want to ground the canoe, so you turn back toward the dock. Your movement sends a small rippling wave toward the tiny boat and pushes it sideways where it sticks to the bank, fluttering against the dirt.

You stop.

Someone's vow is in there, and wherever they are, you have a sense that they are hurting and that you must read their vow. You paddle toward the little boat, running the canoe against the sandy bottom, and step out into the low, murky water. You walk through the shallow water to the bank, grab the tiny boat now tinged with silt, then turn back to the canoe, where you sit down and read the message within.

I have been in a place where my Electric
had dimmed so low,

That I felt lost in darkness.

A vow is a personal lighthouse,
an oath that electrifies that glow within us
and illuminates our world.

Here is my vow and I wish the same for you:

I vow to be a mirror of love and respect.

I call in the right people to my life,
who respect and love me
at the same deep level that I show them.

Thank you for raising the tide for us all,
dear Witch.

Love, VERONICA

Suddenly, water begins to flow beneath the grounded canoe, nudging then releasing it from the sand. As the boat is rising, you read the vow a second time out loud, then you fold up the paper boat and set it at the bow. The canoe begins to move forward, so you reach for your paddle but there is no need. The current is sending the canoe straight toward the dock.

As you ride the tide toward the dock, you grow warm, even a little shaky. You smile and wrap your arms around yourself, feeling a part of all the vows that you just read and that you are a part of something bigger, something collectively beautiful in the universe.

When you reach the dock, you secure the canoe to a post with a rope. Taking the paper boat from the bow, you step onto the dock. A few feet ahead on the weathered boards is a tiny paper boat decorated to match the swirls and magick symbols of your canoe and adorned with gold glitter spelling your name. A black fine-tipped marker lies beside it. You sit down, placing the boat with my message within next to you.

You take the pen and write:

I am filled with the power and glory of the night sky, of the rushing river, of the beauty of nature. I am connected to the vital thread of humankind, of sisterhood and brotherhood, as we navigate this life together.

I vow to stand in my power.

I summon the magickal child that I once was, the strong, radiant being that I am in the present, and the powerful potential of all that I can become in the future.

I vow to respect every version of myself that has ever existed.

You refold the boat, then take both boats to the edge of the dock. Lying down on your stomach and reaching out as far as you can, you place them side-by-side in the water, gently blowing them into motion toward the dozens of tiny paper boats dancing along the river. As you do this, you see yourself in the moonlit water. You are surprised by your own reflection; it's almost as if you are seeing yourself for the first time. The person you see is almost ethereal, calm yet confident. You feel a wave of support, of understanding . . . of love. What you have been seeking from the world was already within you.

And now you know: self-love isn't a selfish act. It is the deep honoring of yourself, an honoring that enables you to extend your love and have that love reflected back to you. Self-love is the rising tide that lifts all the boats on the night river; it is the Electric that powers and flows through us all.

Nikki

Anna

Ahana

Bee

Heather

Nicole

The Spells

SOME DAYS YOUR ELECTRIC SURGES THROUGH you, giving you a supernatural boost that makes you feel weightless, as if gravity itself no longer has command over you. And on grayer days, it can be harder to recall that buoyant vibe. That's why I invented this spell: to revive you with a blast of self-love, helping you see the light on the other side of any darkness you might be going through.

In magickal spells throughout time, the moon has played a central role in illuminating beauty and enhancing power and allure. It is a sacred Bohemian rite to call down the full moon and let her fill your spirit with ancient magick and magnetism. The full moon phase is the optimal time to perform this spell because it is at its magickal peak. The moon is fully present, fully illuminated, and you, my dear Witch, can harness that power.

This spell draws down the full power of the moon by using the energy of the elements in conjunction with crafting a Lighthouse Candle (see page 60 and pages 76–83). You'll call on the ancient mystery of the moon to charm and bless your own sacred temple—your body. Performing these rites is enlivening—it is at its essence what being a Witch feels like, an invigoration of the mind, body, and spirit that comes with holding hands with the natural world and its mysteries.

TOOLS AND MATERIALS

For the Candle

The instructions here utilize a Lighthouse Candle that you carve and anoint yourself, but if you would rather not to do that, you can use a standard seven-day glass candle in either red or white and simply skip Step 2 of the instructions.

- Red seven-day pull-out candle in a glass container
- Carving tool (any clay carving tool, pencil, or small pocketknife)
- Nine drops lemon essential oil
- Two ounces nontoxic gold glitter
- One teaspoon honey or alternative sweetener

For the Spell

- One stick of incense in any scent that you enjoy
- One found feather or one from a craft store
- One large long-stemmed pink rose
- Lighter or matches
- One cup water in a small bowl
- 12-inch length of string

CAST THE SPELL

1. Set the Invitation as instructed on pages 43–47.

2. Use the red candle to make a Lighthouse Candle as instructed on pages 76–83. Carve a large heart on one side and your name on the other. Anoint the candle with the lemon essential oil and adorn it with the gold glitter as instructed on page 81.

3. On the night of a full moon, take the candle, incense stick, feather, pink rose, and bowl of water outside to a spot where you can view the moon clearly, or bring your supplies to a spot by a window where the moonlight reaches.

4. Light the incense stick and hold it in your Spirit Hand (nondominant hand). Take the feather in your dominant hand and waft the incense smoke toward you, starting from the top of your head and moving down toward your feet. As you do this, speak this incantation:

> Smoke of incense, feather of air,
> For my sexy, sultry self-love affair,
> Swirl around me on this night,
> Enchant me by the sweet moonlight.

5. Take the feather, quill facing up, and place it against the outside of the glass container, about an inch below the top. Secure the feather in that position with the string. This helps to further mark your candle as a reminder that you have claimed a new beginning for your own Electric as a result of performing this rite.

6. Light the candle and hold it up to the moon. Speak this incantation in a clear, strong voice:

> Candle be a lighthouse in the dark,
> And in my soul, ignite a spark.
> I am passion, light, and flame,
> Blessed is my very name.

7. Set the candle down in front of you. Take the bowl of water in both hands and hold it up to the moon to imbue the water with luminous energy. Speak this incantation in a powerful voice:

> Beams of Mother Moon upon this water,
>
> Hear me now at your celestial altar.
>
> Droplets touch my skin and shall bless
>
> The beauty, courage, and love I possess.

8. Dip your fingertips in the water and give yourself a moon bath by pressing the water droplets on the top of your head, your third eye (the space between your eyebrows), your throat, behind your earlobes, your heart, your stomach, your sacred parts, your thighs, behind your knees, your calves, and your toes.

9. Take the rose and hold it up to the moon. With power in your voice, say:

> Pink rose of earth, growing wild,
>
> Bestow self-love upon your child.
>
> Remind me when I need it most,
>
> As I hold these petals close.

10. Take the rose and place its petals against your third eye, then slowly drag the flower down the curve of your nose until it is underneath your nostrils. Breathe in the fragrance deeply, then exhale. Repeat breathing in the scent of the flower and exhaling a few times, then drag the rose down the center of your throat and over your heart.

11. Take the petals from the rose and put a few in your underwear. Place the remaining petals in front of you on the ground before your feet.

12. Stand tall with your feet shoulder-width apart. Extend your arms above your head and in a Y shape. Hold your fingertips outstretched to the sky and, without changing the position of your hands, ball your fingers into fists and then release them repeatedly. Speak this incantation to the moon with power in your voice. As you speak, keep balling up and releasing your fists as if you are calling the power of the moon into your hands.

> Mother Moon, I call out to you,
> Fill me with love and keep me true.
> Show me the power that I have inside,
> Beacon of light, my luminous guide.
> Roses at my feet, the world does swoon,
> On this night that I call down the moon.

13. Inhale deeply and place your hands over your heart. Look up at the moon. Imagine her ancient power and magick surging through your skin, increasing your feelings of self-worth and love. Thank the moon, the elements, and the Spirits for supporting you through this ritual.

14. Gather the rose petals at your feet and place them in a small bag.

15. Blow out the candle. Imagine all the incantations that you spoke under the full moon have now transformed into cursive writing in the smoke trails going to the sky for the Spirits to read.

16. In your bedroom, sprinkle the rose petals on your pillow and place your Lighthouse Candle and whatever is left of your moon water on your altar. You may sprinkle the moon water on your magickal tools and items to bless them, and you may relight the candle whenever you need to ignite your own Electric feelings of self-love. When you wake up the next morning, tape the rose petals into your grimoire and record the experience of your moon rite.

SWEET CHILD O' MINE

THERE IS NO MAP OF THE ROAD OF LIFE, AND IT can be easy to feel like you've lost your way. If you're feeling unsure about making a decision or are having trouble seeing next steps toward achieving a goal, this spell summons strong decision-making abilities and a confident sense of direction in such a dynamic way that you will never second-guess yourself again! This spell helps you unlock your inner compass to conjure up the one person who knows what you really want, will hold you accountable, and keep you on course: your inner child, your Little Self.

Little Self.

You will need to perform this spell in a space where you can place a mirror—one large enough to reflect your face—upright and set a candle before it. A small table pushed against the wall is ideal since you will need to sit in front of the mirror to conduct the spell.

TOOLS AND MATERIALS

- Childhood photograph of yourself
- Mirror that you can easily lean against the wall, at least 8 × 10 inches
- Tealight candle
- Lighter or matches
- 9-inch ribbon that matches the color of something you are wearing in the photo
- Box of crayons

CAST THE SPELL

1. Set the Invitation as instructed on pages 43–47.

2. On a small surface with a wall directly behind it, place the mirror so it leans against the wall. Take your childhood photo and lean it against the mirror so the image faces you. Place the tealight candle a few inches in front of the photo.

3. Light the candle.

4. Sit down in front of the mirror to perform the following incantation. You will repeat it three times. The first time, speak in a whisper, as if you are waking your Little Self from a nap. The second time, imagine that your Little Self is awake now, so speak in a clear, determined voice. The third time, raise the energy for the spell by speaking loudly and with command.

> As I light this candle flame,
> I call the one who shares my name.
> Whisper to me what we should do,
> To call in our power and stay true.

5. Look into the eyes of your Little Self in your childhood photograph, then inhale and exhale slowly and deeply three times.

6. Close your eyes and imagine your Little Self standing in the doorway of the room, overwhelmed with joy at seeing you.

7. Call out your name and imagine opening your arms as your Little Self runs over to hug you. Wrap your arms around your Little Self. Imagine their heart pressed against yours and a deep feeling of safety, love, and joy. As you imagine this scene, wrap your arms around yourself in a hug.

8. Now imagine a wave of light moving through your heart that fills your spirit with understanding and care. Your Little Self and you know each other better than anyone else. Take a moment and feel how good it is to be understood completely and loved unconditionally.

9. When you are ready, tell your Little Self about your situation. You can open your eyes and look at the photo or you can keep your eyes closed and imagine your Little Self standing before you, listening to you and holding your hands. Describe the pros and cons of the different paths that you might take. Spill it. Say everything. Your Little Self will never judge you. Talk it all out. Once you have relayed all, end with a clear question in this concise format: "Should I [first option] or should I [second option]?"

10. How does your Little Self react? Can you feel it in your body or see it in your mind's eye right away? Your Little Self will help you make the decision by giving you a gut feeling toward one or the other.

11. Imagine your Little Self hugging you tightly. Feel their love, support, and care. They want what is best for you and are invested in your ultimate happiness. Imagine your Little Self giving you a kiss on the cheek and letting you know that you have their love and support and that they are always there for you. They are so happy that you called for them!

12. Open your eyes and look at the photo. Take the ribbon and tie it in a bow around your wrist or your neck and wear it for three consecutive days to remind yourself of your commitment to stay true to yourself. As you tie the knot, speak this incantation to seal the spell:

> With this knot I make a choice,
> Guided by my own past voice.
> I stand true to the life I desire,
> Seal this spell with breath of fire.

13. Put your face near the candle as if you were going to blow it out. Instead, suck in your breath as if you were inhaling the power of fire and then blow it out to send the smoke trails of your incantations to the sky, where the Spirits and your Guardians can read them and make them so.

14. Imagine your Little Self jumping into your arms and embracing you with love and courage on your path. Say aloud:

> See it. Be it. So be it.

15. Leave the box of crayons in front of the photo as a present for your Little Self. Keep the photo, the mirror, the tealight, and the crayons in place for three days. If you feel compelled to color with the crayons, go for it! It's your Little Self wanting to play!

WHEN YOU SAY "YES" TO WHO YOU TRULY are, all the doors will open. When you fall in love with yourself, the world falls in love with you. There is an old saying, "Energy flows where attention goes." When your Electric is flowing within you, when that bright illumination of self-love is on, the world takes notice. Performing this vow of self-devotion is essential to obtaining the courage and power to perform the spellcasting in this book. This self-marriage ceremony unleashes the vital personal energy you need to wield your own Electric, and it will help you perform all the spells in this book with more power. It will also electrify your magnetism, drawing those you wish to attract to you in relationships and friendships.

At Witch Camp, we perform our self-marriage ceremony as a group. We all walk down to the river and wade in. We marry ourselves at the same time, cheering one another on and throwing rose petals at one another after we declare our individual self-love vows.

The fun part is that you get to pick your own ring and your own look, and your judgmental Great-Aunt Ruth isn't going to be commenting about it! Your dress can be anything from a tattered vintage slip draped in pearls to a button-up white shirt and a black tie. Dress your fantasy! Your ring can be anything that makes you feel wonderful, from a splurge on a sparkler to a kitschy mood ring. One of my favorite rings belonged to Ruby, whose wedding band was a little black adjustable ring shaped like a bat!

Let your Electric self-love sizzle set your style. Your commitment to yourself should be done your way. Step up to the altar of you, my darling Witch, and say, "I do."

- ✦ Three red roses
- ✦ Thirteen tealight candles
- ✦ A ritual adornment (beautiful necklace, flower crown, or accessory that makes you feel incredible when you wear it)
- ✦ Small altar (see page 234)
- ✦ 8½ × 11-inch piece of writing paper (thirty-two pound)
- ✦ Pen
- ✦ 6-inch piece of twine or ribbon

- ✦ Your wedding attire (clothing that fully expresses who you are)
- ✦ Three 8-inch taper candles: one yellow, one orange, one red
- ✦ Three candleholders
- ✦ Ring of your choice
- ✦ Small bell
- ✦ Lighter or matches
- ✦ Your favorite three sentences you created when you performed the Crossfire Hurricane Spell (page 114)

CAST THE SPELL

1. Choose your special date. The date you pick is like a new birthday but even more powerful because it's the day that you will commit to your own power and passion.

2. Decide on the ceremony space. You can perform it in your bedroom, in a dreamy nature spot, or anywhere you feel strong. Where is a power spot for you?

3. Decide on attendees. You can send out invitations to friends to witness your ceremony, or you can do it solo.

4. Set the Invitation as instructed on pages 43–47.

5. Draw a ritual bath with rose petals scattered from one of the three roses. Place thirteen tealights around the bathtub. In Bohemian magick, it is customary to take ritual baths naked but adorned (the adornment is what differentiates a ritual bath from a regular bath in Czech Romani culture). Take off your clothes and adorn yourself with a beautiful necklace, bracelets, a flower crown, or whatever makes you feel divine. If you don't have a bathtub, a shower will do. The core intention is to pamper yourself. You can place the rose petals at your feet in the shower and set the tealights on a counter in your bathroom.

6. Let the calming water soothe your mind, and begin to fantasize about your wedding vows. What gorgeous practices, acts, and ideas do you want to commit to? They can be sexy, creative, mystical, and adventurous. Have fun with it!

7. When you are done with your ritual bath or shower, imagine the water going down the drain carrying away anything that you no longer need. Dry yourself off and slip into something comfortable.

8. It's time to write your magickal vows. Traditional vows like "I vow to honor, to love, and to cherish myself" can be a good place to start. You can also add spice by creating your own, for example,

> I vow to indulge my wild creative spirit, to adventure boldly, and to bewitch my days with music, art, poetry, love, and sex magick. I vow to see the best in me and the best in others.
> I vow to know, without a doubt, that my time here is precious, and I will spend it on things that are worthy, exciting, awe-inspiring, passionate, and nurturing.

Put on music you love and write your vows. Take your time. When you are satisfied with them, scroll the paper toward you, as the vows written upon it are something you want to bring to you. Tie the scroll with ribbon or twine, then set it aside to bring with you to your ceremony.

9. Change into your wedding attire.

10. In the ceremonial place of your choosing, set up a small altar. This can be a small table, a tree stump, or even a piece of cloth to set your ceremonial things on. Place the three taper candles in their candleholders in a row that sits at the edge of the altar that is farthest away from you. They should sit in this order, from left to right: red, orange, yellow. Slide your ring onto, or place it in front of, the red candle for vibrant self-love and passion.

11. Place two red roses in the middle of the altar with their stems crossing in the shape of the letter X. Beneath the roses, place the scroll of your vows. Place the bell beneath the scroll of your vows and closest to you.

12. Imagine four powerful Witches holding their arms to the sky to cast their spell as rain pours down and lightning bolts flash. That's the vibe you want! Now it's your turn to cast the spell. You are the powerful Witch in this story. Stand tall and hold your arms up to the sky like you own it. Let your personal power radiate through your speaking voice and declare your arrival!

```
             I am
        [full name],

          born under
       [zodiac sign],

          ruled by
      [ruling planet],

         born of the
[desert plains / high mountains /
 wild forests / ocean shores / etc.].
```

Add your three favorite sentences that you wrote in the Crossfire Hurricane spell on page 114. Continue:

```
On this day, the [date, month, and year],
I make an eternal vow to myself. With the
ringing of this bell, I call my supportive
Ancestors and my guiding Spirits to witness
            this ceremony.
```

Ring the bell.

13. Light the red candle, then light the orange and the yellow candles from the red candle's flame. Recite this incantation in the gender appropriate to you:

```
Girl that I was, Woman that I am,

     Goddess that I become,

I ignite the fires of love in the colors
        of the rising sun.

With all the versions of me, I call back
          my power now,

I summon up my Electric Wild with the
        voicing of this vow.
```

PRIMA
ESPOSIZIONE INTERNAZIONALE D'ARTE MODERNA DECORATIVA
TORINO · APRILE · NOVEMBRE · 1902 · SOTTO L'ALTO PATRONATO DI S.M. IL RE D'ITALIA

LEONARDO BISTOLFI—TURIN.   PLAKAT DER AUSSTELLUNG ZU TURIN. 1902. (¼ NAT. GRÖSSE).

14. Take the scroll from your altar and untie the twine or ribbon. Read your vows out loud, ignited with your power and passion. The confidence with which you speak this spell is the confidence that will continue to radiate in your life.

15. Once you have read your vows, say:

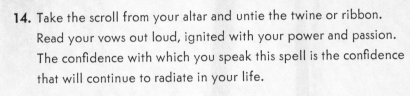

I place this ring upon my finger as a reminder of my vow

and commitment to myself and my own Electric Wild.

As I blow out the candle that holds my ring,

the smoke sends my vows to be written in the stars for all time.

Blow out the red candle. Slide the ring off the candle and onto your finger.

16. Pull the petals off one rose. Cup the petals with your palms together, hold your hands to the sky, and shower the petals all over the top of your head and body.

17. Stand strong and hold your arms to the sky. State the following with determination:

Beginning on this day and for eternity,

I claim my OWN Electric.

It belongs to me.

This body is a divine temple.

I give myself

FULL UNRESTRAINED PERMISSION

to fall madly, to fall deeply,
to fall wildly in love

With my body

With my mind

With my soul

With my being.

This creates the foundation for my
juicy, luscious life.

The Legendary Love that runs through
me is eternal.

I am beautiful. I am beloved.
And I am BADASS.

Go and tell that.

18. Blow out the orange candle to seal your declaration.

19. Thank the Spirits and those who gathered to witness your vow. Blow out the yellow candle to send your gratitude to them through the smoke going up to the sky.

20. Take the last rose and give it to someone who could use the power, love, and energy that is locked into it. You can give it to someone you know, or you can pass it to a stranger on the street. This is symbolic of building yourself up and then spreading the good love and energy to others to make the world a better place.

21. If you performed the ceremony outside your home, create a special altar space (see page 234) inside your home when you return. Put the red, orange, and yellow candles in this special place where they will not be disturbed. Light them for an hour every day for the next seven days. When they are lit, consider this time your Electric Wild hour and do things that promote your self-love. You can work on one of your dreams, put on music and dance up a storm, read your vows aloud again, write in your grimoire, dress up, or whatever makes you feel inspired and good about yourself! When the candles have burned down completely, take the wax and wrap it in a cloth or put it in a resealable bag and place it under your mattress so you can continue to get these juicy vibes while you sleep.

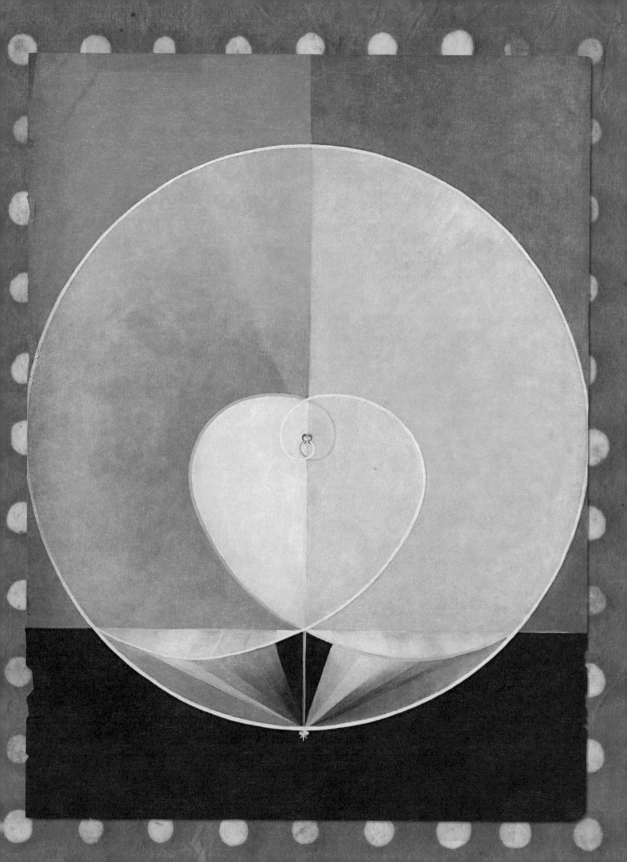

INITIATION IV

======

LOVE MAGICK

WHEN YOU DEVOTE YOURSELF TO LOVE AND sensuality, you illuminate the divine in you and emanate it to the world around you. Sensuality is its own secret language. If you learn the ways to speak it fluently, you will have the eternal key to a luscious love life.

The secret spells of Initiation IV open the portals of pleasure. You will create a crystal-and-rose love crown to draw someone to you who possesses the three traits you most value in a partner, and you will perform a devotional love ritual using Bohemian knot magick, candle magick, and storytelling enchantments. Be prepared to play, unleash your sensual side, and fling open the doors for your own temple of love. The core secret to love spellcasting is to set a clear intention in your mind for exactly what it is that you want.

"It's all about knowing what you want!" Contessa sings out as she hands each of us an elegantly mismatched Victorian teacup filled with her legendary rosehip tea, steeped with rosehips she forages herself, as she sings to them with secret rhyming incantations. The tea tastes as though you are drinking a love spell!

Silvana raises her teacup in a toast: "To knowing what we want—and to getting it!"

We clink our teacups together and throw our heads back and howl because that's just what we do at Witch Camp.

"Pinkies out!" Heather, our elegant Witch sister from London, laughs as we all stick our pinkies out and sip the sweet warm sensual tea.

There are thirteen of us sprawled out on the floor together, surrounded by tall, thin taper candles, while we take turns telling each other juicy love stories. We each packed a favorite vintage slip, flowing dressing gown, or vibrant silk robe to wear for our Witch Camp Tea and Tarot Night. Ruby surprises us by unpacking a trunk of her handmade velvet capes to play dress-up, and we take turns wrapping ourselves in lush capes in rich red, vibrant orange, forest green, and dusty gray.

Before us on the floor are red velvet roses on wire stems, thin gold headbands, and a wooden bowl filled with raw aura quartz crystals soaking in saltwater. The crystals have been charging in the rays of the moonlight and sunlight since everyone arrived twenty-four hours ago.

I tell them the Witches' secret love spell-crafting mission for the evening is to pick their three favorite crystals to adorn a love spell crown. Each sparkling aura crystal must represent a nonnegotiable trait they want to manifest in a love relationship.

We go around the room, each Witch throwing out one of their own nonnegotiable traits in a partner.

"Sex!" yells Ruby. "It's got to be otherworldly, deep, connected, present, and playful."

"Magick!" Nicole chimes in. "I want a partner who understands my magick and wants to join in and explore with me. Tarot cards, doing spells, all of that."

"Art!" says Jen. "My partner and I bond over art and music and it's our way of communicating with each other."

"Adventure!" Heather calls out. "I love traveling and seeking out new places and exploring. I love that my husband enjoys it just as much as I do."

"Trust!" says Kristi. "She's got to be someone who I can have solid communication with, someone who is truthful and honest."

The room is full of vibrant energy as everyone sips the last of Contessa's rosehip tea. The Victorian teacups are scattered on the floor. The time has come to take our night walk in the forest to the river, letting our lanterns illuminate our path. This has become a tradition at Witch Camp, especially when we need to get our minds focused to set our solid, clear intentions for a spell. The Witches have a lot to think about as they pick the three nonnegotiable traits they want in their love relationship, and a silent walk in the night woods always helps uncover the answers!

I take thirteen tall, thin taper candles and pass one to each Witch. I light mine and touch the wick to Silvana's, who touches her wick to Sage's, and so on, until that one flame has been multiplied and passed to all of us in a domino effect. We each gather a golden lantern from the dining room table. We open the tiny seven-inch doors on the front of the lanterns and nestle our candles in the holders inside.

We emerge through the circular hobbit door into the night, each of us holding our lanterns in one hand, and three of the aura crystals in the other. The fragrant summer air moves around us as we make our way to the forest path, a curving line of strong women, Witches with their minds brewing with solid foundations of love.

Contessa gathering rosehips for her magickal tea.

The Journey

THE EARLY EVENING FOG HANGING IN THE AIR is heavy and humid as the sky grows darker. A rolling mass of gray clouds, both light and dark, form like the cigarette smoke seeping out of the blues clubs on this old and narrow cobblestone street lit by ornate wrought-iron gas lamps. Up ahead, over a bar, a hot-pink neon sign buzzes to you from a window that is otherwise dark: LOVE SPELLS & TAROT CARDS. Suddenly, the clouds open up and rain splatters down quickly in warm, thick drops, so you run for the bar door and once inside decide to follow your curiosity up the rickety stairs to the tarot parlor on the second floor, which is candlelit.

Water drips down your face as you pull open the worn wooden door, its jingling brass bell announcing your entry. The exotic smell of rich jasmine incense welcomes you as the vibrant, sensual energy of the tarot reader's parlor draws you further in. On a table a few feet before you, a rich purple and red silk cloth spills across its surface, and upon the cloth stand numerous candles of varying sizes, lit with flames high and flickering, their wax a brilliant blood red. At the table, there are two Victorian high-backed mahogany chairs, their arms engraved with tiny roses, their seats and backs covered in rich red velvet. The chair closest to the door seems to have been pulled out from the table for you. You take a seat, resting your arms on the well-worn fabric.

In a moment, she arrives, moving through a beaded fuchsia curtain that parts without a sound and dances in her wake. You hear music now, Frank Sinatra crooning "Witchcraft," slow and soothing. As she emerges from the candlelit shadows, you see her peroxide-blonde curls first and then, in contrast to her pale skin, her bright red lipstick. She lights a cigarette and takes a deep drag, exhaling rings of pink smoke, looking right at you all the while.

You can feel her hazel eyes on you, reading something deep within you. You know who she is. She's been dead for decades, but in the haunted nooks and alleys of New Orleans, anything is possible. In the light of this candlelit place, she seems very much alive.

Helen be thy name.

A smile moves across her face. "Welcome, child. I was wondering when you were going to get here. I've been waiting for you." She takes a soft red velvet cape from an antique coat rack and moves toward you, wrapping it around your shoulders. "Here, now, dry off. Get cozy and settle in. Let's peek into the cards and do a love reading for you, yes? Maybe a love spell even?"

"That sounds great," you say. "Give me all of it."

The two of you laugh out loud, and it feels easy, friendly, like you've known each other forever. She sits down in the matching chair across the table from you. With turquoise and silver rings decorating each of her fingers, she places her right hand on the tarot cards and then fans them before you in an arch like a crescent moon.

You hover your hand an inch above the sapphire blue cards decorated with golden stars. Your hand trembles a bit with excitement as you make a full, slow sweep across them, then you pass back over them a second time. Some strange supernatural pull happens as your hand feels suddenly heavy and drops on a card near the center. Your pointer finger traces the back of that card and slides it out from the rest. You look up to catch Helen's eyes as you slowly turn the card faceup.

On the card is a woman with a crown of stars on top of her head, draped seductively across a fiery orange and red throne. She appears to smile at you as she holds a scepter high in her right hand, the emblem of Venus etched in stone beside her.

Helen whistles, "Well, will you look at that! The Empress. The Goddess of Love in the tarot. The card of sensuality, of playfulness, of pleasure. The forest is her home. She is in tune with the ways of nature and the ways of herself. That's the essence of a Witch. Look how she holds herself, child. See how she radiates power? That's a woman who knows exactly what she wants and is alive with her pleasure."

Helen exhales a perfect smoke ring into the air, leans over the table, and brings her voice to a low whisper, "She represents a part of you. You chose that card because it is time for you to call in that power. Love. Sensuality. Knowing exactly what you want." She snaps her long fingers, her nails painted a glittering crimson, "I know just the spell you need, child."

She winks as she gracefully glides from her chair to a gleaming red-lacquer cabinet in the corner. She carefully gathers mystical items from the shelves as she sings along with Ol' Blue Eyes.

You hold the Empress card beneath the candlelight. The soft glow illuminates the card's details—the golden sky, the deep blue waterfall, the vibrant forest, and her smile, strong and seductive.

Helen sits back down across the table from you, her cigarette perched in the V between her index and middle fingers. "I want you to make a wish on that candle as you are looking at that Empress card. See the wish clearly in your mind and blow out the candle when you are ready."

As you look at the Empress card, you think of how you truly want to rise in your own power of love, to be both sensual and strong, to be brave and to know exactly what you want. You imagine yourself sitting on the throne of the Empress card, a crown upon your head.

You blow your wish to the flame, and it flickers out to transform into cursive smoke for the Spirits to read and, when the time is right, fulfill.

The room glows with the pink neon cast from the sign outside the window as Helen opens her hand to show you three raw aura quartz crystal points. They glow like tiny wands of light in her palm.

She taps a long finger on the crystals. "These quartz crystals are the bones of the earth. Stones and crystals hold the stories. They are ancient beings and can amplify your desires for you if you ask them to. You have three wishes, one for each crystal, and each wish will be a trait that you desire in your true love relationship. And just like when you made a wish on the candle, you must think of a clear wish for each crystal. Whisper it to the crystal as your words imbue it with power and ignite it into being with your breath."

She places the three crystals into your hands, and you feel the warmth of the crystals vibrating through your palms.

"Choose those three traits wisely, child. Choose the three traits of a true love relationship that will last through the gorgeous days of your life. When you know what you want and you are clear, the magick can find you more easily."

Helen touches the top of your head with the palm of her hand and strokes your hair as you think, and suddenly it feels like everything in the world is exactly how it should be. The comforting sensation of her gentle hand covered in turquoise and silver rings on the crown of your head is soothing and warm. You feel a peace and a clarity that you have not known in a long time.

"Thank you, Helen." You hear your voice come out of your mouth in tones both strong and kind, almost enchanted. You feel a supernatural charge of energy around her as if she is sharing her strength, love, and sensual languor just by being in the room.

She places a small red velvet drawstring pouch before you. Its contents include a gold headband, golden wire, and her handwritten instructions for the spell.

"With the crystals in your hand and the contents of this pouch, you will craft a love spell crown. It is time to rise in your love divinity, child, just like the Empress from the stories of the tarot. Now, put your crystals in this pouch and take these four red roses for your crown—one for you, one for your true love, and two for the Spirits who watch over you both. Four also symbolizes the four strong corners of a house. May love be your home for all time."

She holds out four red roses and their sweet scent fills the air in the little tarot parlor. You are moved to hug her, and when you do, a feeling washes over you of being truly seen and cared for by this magickal Grandma. You take the roses and breathe in their aroma as she puts her hands on your shoulders.

"I stand by you as you feel your power growing stronger with each passing day. You are alive, sweet child, and in you, in these initiations you take, you keep the old Bohemian Magick traditions alive." She places the red velvet spell pouch in your palms, "Thank you. Thank you for not letting them forget us."

"Never," you say.

You move toward the door. Your hands push against the glass and the bells jingle as you turn around to say goodbye. Her eyes glint with tears as she smiles and says, "Look at you, child of Spectaculus magick and the Wild. I'm proud of you."

You smile back, radiating with a sense of true belonging while you carry on this long legacy of Bohemian Witches.

Before you can answer, she continues, waving toward the pink neon, "I should tell you that this sign—well, only the ones who are meant to see it, see it. There's nothing here but a dark, deserted second floor to most people's eyes. But the mystics and the artists and the seekers and the Witches . . . we have a different way of seeing, don't we?"

She winks.

"Yep, pink neon," you say.

"Pink neon forever," she laughs.

You push open the door and head down the stairs to the cobblestone street, holding the red velvet spell bag of your love crown and the four blood-red roses triumphantly in your hand. The air is clear; a sea of stars crowns the old Crescent City, and you feel more alive than you've felt in a long time. You hear the sounds of sultry blues, and people are spilling out onto the sidewalks from the clubs, kissing, holding each other close.

You let go and start to dance as you walk. You feel alive. Truly alive. Like your story is just beginning. You are a Witch with a love spell crown in a red velvet bag dancing down the streets of New Orleans. You laugh and throw your head back to look at the moon, and as you do a faint smoke ring tinged in pink hovers above you, then dissipates into the night sky.

The Spells

―――――

THERE IS a LIGHT THAT NEVER GOES OUT

THIS WITCH "CRAFTING" RITUAL USES CRYSTALS to increase your love mojo and confidence by helping you to define more clearly what you want in a relationship. After all, nothing is sexier than someone who knows what they want and takes action to get it!

If you are single, this spell works to draw someone to you who has the traits you feel are important. If you are in a relationship, this powerful spell not only reminds you what specific traits are important to you in the relationship but also enhances those traits to keep the connection vibrant and bright. To have a legendary love, you must tend to it; you must see the gems in your relationship and take action to bring them to light. Remember: choose three love traits that will be the strong foundation of a love that will last.

Old Bohemian folklore says that crystals and rocks are the bones of the earth. Crystals hold the ancient stories within them, and if you charge them by placing them in a bowl of saltwater under the light of both the sun and the moon, you can whisper to them what you wish for. The belief is that they will work like magnets to draw your desire to you.

First, define three traits that are important to you in a relationship. Once you have selected them, you'll enchant the crystals by charging them with your wishes. Finally, you will create a beautiful, light-catching crystal-and-rose crown that you can wear as a powerful talisman while performing rituals and spells.

TOOLS AND MATERIALS

- Plastic fabric-covered headband
- Three raw aura quartz crystal points, 1¼ to 3 inches long, with holes drilled through them
- A small bowl with a liquid capacity of one cup
- One cup of water

- Two teaspoons sea salt
- Wire cutters
- One spool of one millimeter, eighteen-gauge, tarnish-resistant copper jewelry wire
- Tape measure
- Dressmaker's chalk
- Four silk or velvet red roses with 5-inch wire stems

PREPARE TO CAST THE SPELL

Before you begin the spell, you need to prepare the crystals. Do this on a night between the new moon and the full moon (any type of weather is fine) since that is when the moon is increasing in its energy and power. You want to draw on that power for this love ritual.

To cleanse the crystals, place them in a small bowl filled with the water mixed with the sea salt. Set the bowl outside on a window ledge or another place where it can receive twelve hours of sunlight and twelve hours of moonlight consecutively. This provides a beautiful balance of energy as it honors the joyous light of the sun and the dark sensual mystery of the moon.

CAST THE SPELL

1. Set the Invitation as instructed on pages 43–47.

2. Once you have cleansed and prepared the crystals for the ritual as instructed in "Prepare to Cast the Spell," sit down in a comfortable, quiet place and take the crystals into your palms. As you hold them, close your eyes and think of the three most important qualities you desire in a love relationship. Consider which traits will bring you and the relationship vibrancy, happiness, fun, and connection even fifty years in the future. If you have a partner, consider your favorite three traits of the relationship and imagine those being enhanced. Allow your imagination to run free as you choose these three important traits. Don't censor yourself; choose what is vital to you.

3. When you are ready, bring the crystals up to your lips and say out loud the three traits of your ideal love relationship and partner. You may add details to how each trait works in your love relationship. For instance, if one of your traits is trust, you can add, "My partner and I have clear, honest communication with each other. We both feel safe in our relationship because our bond of trust is strong. This acts as a solid foundation for us to grow." The crystals act like magnets, drawing to you the story of the love life you wish to have or amplify. Once you have told each crystal the story that it will hold and strengthen for you, take a deep breath and exhale, blowing onto the crystals to share with them the power of your vibrant life force.

4. Now, place all the tools and materials listed for this ritual on a table in a comfortable, well-lit area.

5. The headband will be your crown, so instead of wearing it customarily, with the top of the band extending across the top of your head, you will wear it with the top of the band extending across your forehead. Lay the headband down on the table before you, with the center top facing upward.

6. With a tape measure and chalk, mark the center point of the headband. Then mark the headband about one half inch to the left and right of that center point. These are the three points at which you will attach the crystals.

7. With the wire cutters, cut three 18-inch-long pieces of wire, one for each crystal.

8. Pick up the first crystal and a piece of wire. Thread half of the wire through the drilled hole.

9. Place the crystal on the headband at the rightmost point. Position the crystal so its point is facing upward and outward, like the right arm of the letter Y. Wrap the wire that you have threaded through the hole around the base of the crystal and headband to join them and to secure the crystal in place.

10. Wrap the remaining wire around the base of the crystal and headband to secure tightly. Tuck the ends of wire under the crystal to prevent them from scratching your forehead when you wear the crown.

11. With the second crystal and wire, repeat steps 8, 9, and 10, positioning the second crystal on the center chalkmark of the headband, with the pointed side facing downward toward your third eye.

12. With the third crystal and wire, repeat steps 8, 9, and 10, positioning the crystal so that it faces upward, like the left arm of the letter Y.

13. About three inches from the center of the crystal Y formation, wrap two rose stems around the headband so that the flowers sit side by side and are firmly attached. Repeat with two additional roses three inches on the other side of the center crystal formation. Secure with additional wire if needed.

14. Once you have finished the crystal-and-rose crown, stand or sit in front of a mirror. Place the crown on your head so the center crystal hangs between your eyebrows. Repeat this incantation three times in a powerful voice:

Three points of crystals and red roses four,
I hold the key to open Love's door.
By the powers of air, earth, water, and fire,
Conjure the love life that I desire.
The words I speak cast an auditory potion,
For our love to be poetry and deep devotion.
See it. Be it. So be it.

Your crown is now charged with your words, your desires, and the light of the moon and the sun. When you crown yourself in your spells and your clear intentions, true magick arises.

I MELT with YOU

O CAST THE SENSUAL SPELLS OF LOVE SORCERY, you have a sacred commitment to honor and elevate your love relationship with ritual, ceremony, and the Wild within you. Set aside an enchanted evening to perform this passionate ritual and to create a deep bond between you and your beloved as you cook up a love spell designed to set the night on fire!

I Melt with You combines candle magick and the traditional Bohemian practice of working with the magickal essence of oils, spices, herbs, and flowers to elevate your connection with your beloved. In Spectaculus Witchcraft, we acknowledge that spices, herbs, and flowers are a gift from the natural world and hold vibrant life-force energy that can boost our spellworkings. When you chant this spell's incantations with your lover, mixing your voices together with the poetry of magick, the words will create a powerful purpose for your relationship as you express the blessing bestowed by each flower, herb, and spice.

TOOLS AND MATERIALS

- Two 7-inch red taper candles
- Carving tools (any clay carving tool, pencil, or small pocketknife)
- Citrus oil (orange, lemon, lime, or grapefruit)
- 8-inch pie plate
- One ounce rosebuds or the petals from two red roses
- Nine cinnamon sticks
- One ounce dried orange peel
- Two ounces nontoxic red glitter
- Lighter or matches
- *Optional:* 12 × 12 inch cloth or one-gallon resealable plastic bag

CAST THE SPELL

1. Set the Invitation as instructed on pages 43–47.

2. Get comfortable with your beloved on a blanket or pillows on the floor, sitting cross-legged across from each other with your knees touching. Press your right palm to your lover's heart and your left palm to your own heart. They will mirror you, by pressing their right palm to their heart and their left palm to yours. Take a moment to let your breathing synchronize. Let the intimacy of this moment weave its own magick in your hearts. Kiss your partner's third eye. Let them kiss yours.

3. Take one red candle for yourself and give the other one to your lover. Carve your name vertically down the side of your candle, beginning one inch below the top. Your lover should do the same, carving their own name.

4. Add your Sorcery Signatures: Lick your name on your own candles to add your DNA to the spell.

5. Ask your lover to hold out their dominant hand to you, palm facing up. Put nine drops of citrus oil upon their palm, and as you rub it in be mindful of your intention to create bright vitality and happiness in your union. Your lover will then rub the oils from their palm onto your red candle.

6. Next, hold your dominant palm face up and out to your lover. They should place nine drops of citrus oil into your palm and rub it in with the same intent described in the previous step. Then you will anoint their red candle.

7. Place the candles side by side in the middle of the pie plate before you. Take a lighter and wave the flame under the base of each candle so the wax melts and forms a small puddle on the plate. Stand the candles up and push them into the hot wax, holding them upright until they set.

8. Together, split the rosebuds between you and take an equal amount in each of your hands. Speak this incantation and those that follow powerfully. Say this incantation three times as you both scatter the roses in a ring around the two candles:

> A circle of roses to enchant our love,
> root in the ground and rise high above.

9. Together, place nine cinnamon sticks around the two candles, arranging them like rays of the sun, then say the following three times:

> Cinnamon sticks spark the fire,
> ignite our deep sensual desire.

10. Together, scatter the dried orange peel inside the ring of roses around the base of the candles and say three times:

> Dried orange peels to bring delight,
> from break of day to starry night.

11. Pull the wicks of the candles toward each other and light them at once from a single flame. Together, say three times:

> Fire of passion, spark the flames,
> ignite the two candles that bear
> our names.

12. As the candles begin to burn, sprinkle the red glitter onto them and watch the flames pop and spark. Together, say three times:

> Blessings and enchantments for
> legendary love,
> rain of glitter from above.

13. Now it's time to enchant your bedroom. Bring the two burning candles on the pie plate to a safe place at the foot of your bed.

14. Get in bed and kiss slowly. Take your time to explore each other, looking into each other's eyes while you caress each other. Kiss your lover's earlobes, neck, and mouth. Have them do the same to you. Make love slowly as the candles burn down at the foot of your bed.

15. When the candles have completely burned down, you will have a red wax pie with the roses, the orange peels, and the cinnamon sticks all held within. Take the cooled wax pie out of the pie plate and place it under your mattress. To avoid staining the underside of your mattress, wrap the wax in a cloth or seal in a resealable bag. The beauty of this powerful love spell will keep you both enchanted nightly as you sleep atop your candle-wax love spell.

COME ON, SWEETHEART,

LET'S ADORE

ONE ANOTHER

BEFORE THERE IS

NO MORE

OF YOU AND ME.

—RUMI, Thirteenth Century

There is a place in between time
A place where you and I meet
In a crescent city
Under a crescent moon
Where we fly down the streets
like ghosts.

The slow molasses of your smoky voice
rises in the heat of a Louisiana Afternoon
Your songs summoned on steel strings
Your soles bare and pressed to the ground
Tapping the wooden floor boards
of a 100 year old house on Port Street.

Sweet lady Day gives Herself to Night
like I give myself to you
Naked in Knee socks
Howling for my Magick Man
In the twisted sheets of a borrowed bed
You and I converge to conjure the Cosmos.

In the oldest tree of Congo Square
Strands of our hair entwine
Red wax and roses   *
Rum and cigarettes
Our tongues touch
Under a dozen curving wooden Arms
of a 300 year old tree
And Now
My Soul
Recognizes every Incarnation of You.

BOHEMIAN RHAPSODY

BOHEMIAN KNOT MAGICK (YES, AS IN "TYING the knot") invites clear communication about desires and dreams for you and your beloved and engages in the art of sharing stories to create a deep connection. My Grandma Helen's powerful Bohemian knot magick technique is like making a wish on birthday candles, but instead you seal the wish or gratitude into the ribbon by blowing life into it and then sealing it in the knot. This spell guides you by recalling unforgettable memories you and your partner have built together, expressing gratitude for the present, and dreaming up wild, gorgeous wishes for the future.

Giving and receiving is an active process. Open your heart. Be vulnerable. Break down barriers. Invite love in. This ritual is a confession of one soul to another. Honor each other with love and story and truth. Weave a spell of your legendary love.

Grandma Helen
+ Grandpa Warren

David & Me

TOOLS AND MATERIALS

✦ **Six feet of red silk ribbon**

CAST THE SPELL

1. Set the Invitation as instructed on pages 43–47.

2. Get comfortable with your beloved on a blanket or pillows on the floor, sitting cross-legged across from each other with your knees touching. Press your right palm to your lover's heart and your left palm to your own heart. They will mirror you, by pressing their right palm to their heart and their left palm to yours. Take a moment to let your breathing synchronize. Let the intimacy of this moment weave its own magick in your hearts. Kiss your partner's third eye. Let them kiss yours.

3. Take the red silk ribbon and have your beloved hold one end of the ribbon while you hold the other end. You will now be creating your Bohemian Rhapsody ribbon that comes from traditional Bohemian knot magick. To do this, simply say one thing that you are grateful for in your relationship. For example, "I love your sense of adventure and how much fun we have together when we explore." "I'm grateful for the time you set aside for us to do spells like this." "I love how I can be myself around you and you can be yourself around me." "I'm really proud of our clear, honest communication with each other."

4. Once you have shared your love gratitude, make one knot in the ribbon about seven inches from your end while blowing the thought of your gratitude into the knot as you tie it.

5. Now it's your lover's turn. They will now share something they are grateful for in the relationship and then they will tie a knot seven inches from their side of the ribbon, blowing the gratitude into the knot as it is tied.

6. Now it's your turn again. For the rest of this ritual, you have a choice of what to share each time. You can share a love gratitude, a positive memory, a future wish, or blessing. Blow your wish into the ribbon and seal it with your second knot seven inches away from your first

knot. As you and your lover share or make a wish, your knots will move closer together each time, eventually meeting in the center.

7. Now it's your lover's turn to share.

8. Perform this exchange a total of four times each, so that there are eight knots in the ribbon. Take your time and enjoy this ritual. If you want to share a story or a memory of the two of you that connects with your gratitude, then go for it. Sharing stories enhances the connection between the two of you and creates a stronger bond. Once eight knots have been tied, loosely tie the ninth knot in the middle but don't pull yet and speak this incantation together powerfully three times into the ninth loose knot:

> The North, the South, the East, the West,
> My Beloved and I, eternally blessed.
> We stand at the altar of our Love Divine,
> We open the secret portals in between time.
> We call in the sacred power of three,
> The Spirits who watch over us, my beloved and me.
> Immortal lovers, so mote it be.

After you speak this incantation the third time, tie the center knot together as you blow into it. Then meet in the middle for a kiss.

9. Spend slow, quality, connected time gazing into each other's eyes and kissing. When you are ready, decorate the back of your headboard with the Bohemian Rhapsody knot magick ribbon or hang it above your bed. This enchants your bed and is a visual reminder of your love gratitude, happy memories, future wishes, and blessings as a magickal couple.

> See it, be it, so be it!

INITIATION V

The COSMIC COVEN of SPECTACULUS

IN WITCHCRAFT, THERE ARE NO MISTAKES AND NO coincidences; there is only destiny and the synchronicities and signs that are woven into it. Every day that we open our eyes here on earth is a chance to adventure, create magick, and journey with all the Electric and the Wild that lives within us.

This book called to you as a companion, a magickal friend, and a treasury of Witchcraft lost and found. You are not the same person that you were when you opened it: you have been trained in the secret mysteries of the Witch Academy of Spectaculus. Before we go on our final journey in this initiation, I want to share a personal story with you that has all the components we've been talking about throughout these pages. This is a story about my Grandma Helen talking to Spirits and a night visit from a dead rock star who wanted me to pass on a very important message to you.

A veil of opaque smoke snaked through the room, resembling the wispy curls of manufactured fog in a nightclub. Everything else in my bedroom was the same as it always was, except, of course, for the silhouetted specter of a dead rock star in the corner.

I found myself in that strange space of waking and dreaming, where time has no meaning and the ghosts come to visit.

It's just what happens to the women in my family. Speaking to the Spirits is just another thing that's passed down, just like our hazel eyes and our cackling laughter.

As a child, sitting cross-legged on my Grandma Helen's shag carpet, I was initiated into the mysteries of conversing with ghosts. My Grandma held a Lucky Strike in the curves of her fingers like other Witches hold a wand of power. Her peroxide-blonde Marilyn Monroe curls moved into her face as she took a drag and exhaled slow smoke rings to the ceiling in a secret knock on the doors of the dead that only she knew. Animatedly, she sliced her hand through the hot Florida air, speaking aloud to the Spirits as she paced back and forth on the black-and-white checkerboard tiles of her kitchen floor. The music of her voice rose and fell in the symphony of her solo séance.

Grandma Helen had a way with the Spirits just like she had with men: with a single request, they all did her bidding.

When I called out to the Spirits that night from my bedroom, I did so without the aid of a cigarette. I did not pace across a tiled floor, nor did I wave my hands in secret patterns of a sign language I will never know. I simply lowered my voice in the dark to match the same smoky musical cadence of my Grandma's voice.

I do that every time.

I called upon the Spirits that night before I went to sleep because I needed guidance about what I should say at a final Witch Camp ceremony the next day. I needed an inspiring, otherworldly answer. I called upon the Spirits in those times, not unlike the way some people call upon Jesus.

I got Lou Reed.

The deep grooves at the sides of his mouth were visible by the moonlight, as his unmistakable voice broke the silence between us:

"Our lives are a story, man, and what we do with it is called art."

His words, his ghostly communication, just like the lyrics of his songs, jolted through me like a lightning bolt of truth. At our final ceremony at Witch Camp the next day, I relayed his words of wisdom, and now, dear Witch, I pass them on to you. Go and live your story. Make your art. Cast the spell of your life.

GHOSTS

A whiskey-soaked voice from the Velvet Underground filled my small bedroom. Lou Reed was standing, one leg propped against the wall, in the corner by my vanity table. It was as if he were leaning against a lamppost waiting for a bus.

He had been dead for some years.

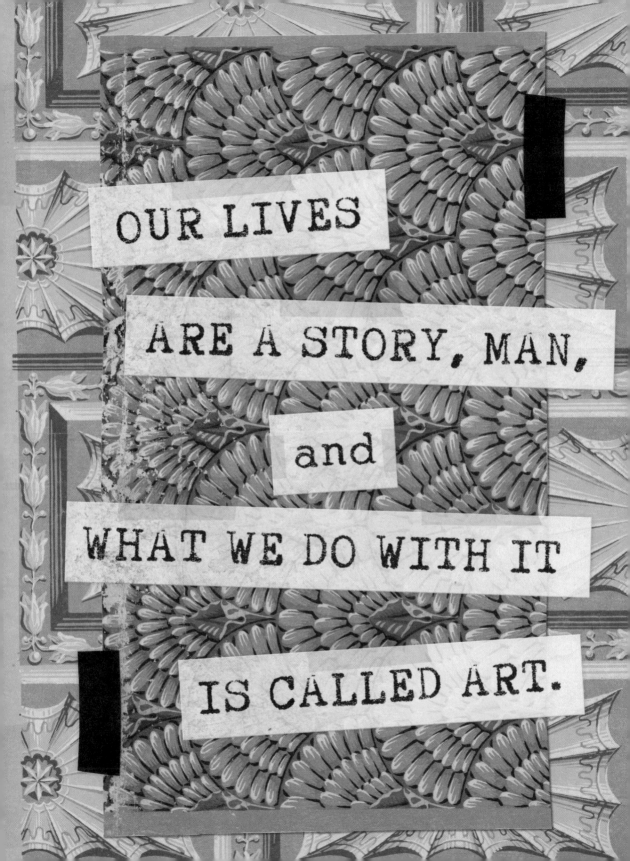

OUR LIVES ARE A STORY, MAN, and WHAT WE DO WITH IT IS CALLED ART.

The Journey

A FLASHBULB POPS. THE LIGHT ERUPTS. WE stick out our tongues, laughing. The flash of light moves through the tiny box room again, and we lean our heads together, our faces beaming big silly grins. The real kind. The kind of smile that illuminates a face and lets you peek into the sunshine of a soul.

This moment is captured in black and white in a strip of four grainy photos. Frozen in time forever.

I pull the dark blue curtain aside and all the light floods in. Neon-pink and lime-green bulbs dangle over the Luna Park midway. The smells of hot buttered popcorn erupting out of its metal basket and of the sizzling dough of funnel cakes on greased grills mix with the saltwater air.

We climb out of the photobooth into the kaleidoscope of a Coney Island night. Our photo strip, still wet with developer, drops into the metal cage on the side of the photobooth. I grab it and tear it across the middle: two pictures for you and two for me. I hide both, enclosing one in each fist, and hold them out in front of me.

"Which one, Witch One?" I ask.

You laugh and slam your palm down on my Spirit Hand like I knew you would. I open it up. It's the last two photos. The bottom strip. The ones of us sticking out our tongues and smiling wildly.

"Awwwww . . . but that's my favorite one," I say.

"Too bad. Shouldn't have put it in your Spirit Hand because it's MINE." You snatch it from my hand.

I grab your arm and start to run down the midway with you toward the rides. AC/DC's "You Shook Me All Night Long" screams from the Musik Express ride. We jump over the metal bars of the line and race to a blue car while the operator is locking the big black safety bars down on the other cars.

While AC/DC sings about American thighs and shaking walls, the ride screeches into action on the rusty track, moving faster, picking up speed until the loud siren wail rips through the air and the whole carnival is a blur of speed and color.

The DJ booms over the loudspeakers:

"DO YOU WANT TO GO BACKWARD???"

We both scream and throw up our hands as the cars lurch backward on the track. I see the look on your face and I think we are probably both thinking, "Yes, we do want to go backward and do our whole journey again because in the unspoken moments of carnival rides and loud music, we both know this is the last initiation."

The loud air horns sound and the ride slowly halts. Dizzy and laughing, I grab your hand and slide out of the car and onto the metal platform to take the steps down to the sidewalk. Bright yellow lights flash around a hand-painted wooden sign that reads BALLOON BLAST WATER RACE with an arrow pointing to the right. We walk down the alleyway as old calliope music moves through the air.

"Step right up, step right up!"

I hear his voice first, then see his gray broad-brimmed hat with a leopard band. His hazel eyes flash against tan skin. "C'MON NOW! We need two more, just two more to have a sold-out game!"

We move up to the last two spots along the bar. He takes our money, and we grab the two water guns, ready to shoot. There are thirteen spots at the bar, each one with a clown head four feet in front of it. We rest our elbows on the counter and get ready to shoot. The bell alarm sounds wildly into the night and streams of water shoot from our guns into the clowns' mouths in front of us and blow up the balloons on their heads. I quickly divert my water stream into your clown's mouth, and the pressure from our two water pistols makes your balloon pop first. It's a little grifting boardwalk trick I learned from my Dad when I was little. He's got his own kind of magick.

You scream out, and the handsome hazel-eyed carny catches my eye and winks. He knows what I did. "Looks like you got the big prize then. Top row." You wait for him to ask you to choose one, but he spins around, grabs a stuffed animal, a bunny with big ears and a heart-shaped face, and puts it on the counter. As he leans across the bar, you notice a pentagram, some kind of handmade wooden circle amulet, and a small corked bottle hanging from three cords around his neck.

I take the little bunny in my arms as we wave goodbye and walk toward the beach. The night waves roll on the sand with a soft *hush hush*, a lullaby among all the noise and chaos of the boardwalk.

"What now?" you ask. You're suddenly tentative. I can tell you're worried about all this ending.

"The Wonder Wheel." The great giant of legend moves through the night sky, 150 feet above the boardwalk. We make our way toward it like a beacon in the night. Screams move through the air in waves under a sign to our left that lights up one letter at a time and then flashes all together: L-O-G F-L-U-M-E.

I turn my face toward you as we walk and say, "My Grandma Irene used to come here when she was a little girl, you know. She asked me if the Wonder Wheel and the Cyclone were still here, and it was nice to say that they still are. So many things change over time, but here we are, in a place of wonder, with two old metal guardians that watch over it still."

We walk around the haunted house that blasts a soundtrack of creaking doors, Witchy cackling, slamming sounds, and howls. The runway for the Wonder Wheel beckons in front of us, lit with red and yellow light bulbs. No one else is on the line. It is almost midnight.

An old man in overalls motions us over and opens the yellow latch on the swinging cage. You slide across the seat, giggling. I hold out the stuffed bunny to you, but I don't step into the cage.

You look at me and you know what's happening. I'm not coming. You know that this initiation, like the others, is one you must do on your own.

"This little bunny is your guide, okay? She won't leave your side. We believe in you."

You take the stuffed bunny with the gigantic ears and the heart-shaped face into your arms. You look at the bunny and look back up at me.

"But how do I get in touch with you?"

"Wait until it's a full moon, then set up thirteen tea lights around a six-foot circle. Lure me in by laying one vintage slip in the center, then scatter rose petals on the fabric. Hold a single sunflower in your Spirit hand and sing Leonard Cohen's 'Suzanne' aloud but use my name instead. I'll hear you."

I wink at you and step back as the old man puts your safety bar down. He cranks the gear and you start to move into the sky. You see me waving up at you from the ground.

I cup my hands around my mouth and shout, "I'm always with you! You hear me? Always!"

Your car keeps climbing until you can't see me anymore and the summer night breeze moves through the safety cage. The entire beach spreads out before you, waves crashing, the skeleton of the old Parachute Drop adorned in lights on the horizon.

The car stops at the very top. As it swings in the silence, the noises below seem far away. You are near the sky, close to the moon, looking over it all.

The world is so far below that you feel like you are looking down at a miniature village with a toy train track running through it. Tiny lights glow from afar. The journeys flash across your mind, all the places you've been since this began: the Midnight Library, the phantom feast, the moonlit river of paper boats, Grandma Helen's supernatural tarot parlor, and here, on the world-famous Wonder Wheel. A sense of peace washes over you, and you hold the stuffed bunny tighter.

But, wait . . .

What is this?

A pocket. A small pocket in the back of the little bunny's neck, hidden under the soft fur.

You open the secret compartment. By the light emanating from the arms of the Ferris wheel, you see a very small bottle with a cork suspended on a thin cord, two baby rosebuds, a small birthday candle, and a tiny scroll. There are four tiny envelopes too, each filled with a different substance: a pinch of cinnamon, a pinch of raw sugar, a teaspoon of calendula, and two pinches of gold glitter.

My darling Witch,

This is an amulet for you to always remember your magick. The tiny bottle is the vessel. I have spoken my own sweet wishes for you into it; they will always be held there. The rest of the ingredients are memories from each Initiation. Hold the bottle in your Spirit hand and sprinkle the gold glitter into the bottom. Take a piece of your hair and put it inside. Put the rosebuds in for love, as this is a love spell for all of your days. Add a bit of calendula for happiness and joy to shine upon you, sugar to keep your life sweet, and cinnamon to keep your passion and creative fire burning for all time.

Take the tiny scroll and write your beautiful name, powerful and bold. Under that, please write: "I am a powerful Witch. I design my destiny. My word is my wand. My voice casts a spell." Put it inside the bottle. Blow upon it. Light the birthday candle and seal the cork with the melting wax. Then hold the bottle up to the sky and say this incantation:

With flower and herb and spice and seed,
A written note for the Spirits to read.
A magnet of magick mojo and love divine,
Come to me, I claim it, for it is mine.
Passion ignites in this love supreme,
Amulet activate, conjure my dream.

You place the ingredients on the seat beside you and follow my instructions from the letter until all the magickal contents are in the amulet bottle. You speak the incantation into the night. You blow your wishes into the top and then hold it up to let the ghosts of Coney Island do the same. The sweet summer breeze moves across the mouth of the bottle, making a low whistle. You feel the Spirits of Coney Island swirl around you. You take the lighter out of your pocket. You strike it alive to light the birthday candle wick; the flame jumps in the breeze but doesn't go out. You hold up the birthday candle, a tiny lighthouse in this night, and as it starts to burn down, you imagine it already building up on the Otherside. You turn the candle sideways, dripping the wax around the cork to seal in all your magick.

You slide the cord around your neck; the amulet falls in front of your heart and rests there. And suddenly you remember—you dig your fingers into your other pocket to find the slick photo strip. In black and white, the two of us smile, side by side for all time, and on the seat beside you, a little bunny with the pocket witnesses it all.

The Road Goes Ever On and On

THIS BOOK IS A LOVE LETTER TO YOU.

To your magick.

To your Wild.

To the Electric that sizzles in your veins.

To the grand mysteries of the secret powers that you hold within you.

Walking the path of Witchcraft and the Wild is a revolutionary act. It is so easy to feel alone in our journey and our experience.

My heart longed for the Witches, for the magick makers, for the cosmic cult of wild visionaries and alchemists to arrive. I knew there were more of us out there, scattered all over the world, people who lived magick, who felt it in some unexplainable space in their soul. This book was my call out to you, that your hands might hold its covers, that your eyes might move across these words. You are not alone.

Thank you for coming on this journey with me, for studying the magick of Spectaculus, for taking a risk and letting yourself be the raw Wild force of nature that you were meant to be. This world so desperately needs your light.

This time that we had together on the pages of this book was deeply personal. As I wrote it to you, to the Witches of the future, to the people who will continue to do good work and make positive changes in our world, I kept the Jack Kerouac quote that I shared with you in the Witch Academy in my mind: "I am writing this book because we are all going to die." What I mean by that is: I wrote this to share my legacy, my family's magick, and the magick that I have found in this world in the loves of my life and in friendships in the hopes that it will help unlock some secrets for you and your journey. I am grateful for the time that you took to walk alongside me in the Wild.

The magic of camaraderie speaks to our bones. Our desire to push past fear and rise to our best lives is a core theme of humanity. We crave the stories of good triumphing over evil, of the underdog taking the lead and rising, of the misfits finding their strength by banding together.

We are all misfits in one way or another. Alone. Misunderstood. Sometimes it can feel as though the obstacles and the odds are against us.

The call of those dreams is the song of our souls.

If this book could pass on a message to you in any way, it would be this: never forget that you have the power inside you to conjure all the very best things to yourself.

Your power has been evident in all the instances you've had in your life that you cannot explain, that seemed like too much of a coincidence, the things you knew in your gut before logic could even process them, the things that came to you in a dream that manifested in your reality, all the things you just *knew*.

We are Witches, after all—revolutions are born in our being.

Our days are a path of our genuine truth, of rising and reclaiming the magick that was lost.

Sometimes you will feel on top of the world, and you will reach out to help your brothers and sisters climb up onto your shoulders and help to make great change. Some days you will feel alone like no one understands you.

Never forget that I am out there. Never forget that there are other magick makers in this family of Spectaculus all over the world, that we call to one another in secret codes like fireflies flashing their bright lights in the darkness.

In our magick, we create a shared worldwide dream of what we can be, of the beauty that is unique in us. While writing this book, I received visits from the Spirits including a Black man named Meslelka who put his hands on my shoulders and told me to "go back to the stake and refuse to die." I listened to him. In this book, I go as far back as I know to share all the old magick. This magick will be printed en masse so no one can destroy us or keep us from speaking, from teaching, from sharing our stories. We will go where they wanted to burn us, and we will refuse to die. All of us. Standing together.

Another dream visit occurred when I was starting to work on this book and this journey with you. A beautiful Mexican woman named Maria told me three powerful words that she carved into the bark of a tree: "Keep it sacred."

Keep it sacred.

In the end, our lives are a story. We become the story. Unfolding for generations after us.

Remember what the ghost of Lou Reed said:

"Our lives are a story, man, and what we do with it is called art."

Share your art with the world.

Live your greatest story.

I will be out here, smiling, knowing that you exist somewhere in this world.

A part of us, that part that felt lost, that felt that empty hole within, is now filled with the knowledge that there are so many of us . . . that we walked this journey together, that this was real and will continue to be real. Never forget our times at the Midnight Library, the moonlit river of paper boats, the phantom feast, our supernatural visit with Grandma Helen, and Coney Island.

They exist.

We are Witches.

We made them real together.

If you need me, close your eyes and imagine getting into your wooden rowboat from Initiation III. Row to me and the other Witches. We are all on this sea of night under an expanding sky of stars. If you close your eyes, you can see us all there, all of us and everyone you've ever loved—all your Ancestors, the Spirits, and the people who made your heart fill with joy during the years of your life. We are all there. Love never dies.

We are stronger than death.

There is no end because there never is.

We all continue on in story.

Our dreams are pieces of puzzles of secret communications of messages from the Guardians, Ancestors, Spirits, and one another. Our magick was the missing piece.

Your magick is your legacy. I pass along this grimoire of the secret magick of Spectaculus to you. Feel it. Rise up and claim all your messy, beautiful magick.

No one can ever take it from you.

You are the heir.

I am the last daughter,
and I was always waiting for you.

SPECTACULUS WORDERY

A POCKET LEXICON

ERE ARE DEFINITIONS OF MAGICKAL WORDS commonly used in this book. Some are phrases I've invented, while others are classic magickal terms and concepts.

✦ **ALTAR:** A dedicated sacred space (usually a shelf or small table) where you can work your magick, light candles, talk to the Spirits, and place ceremonial items.

✦ **ANCESTORS:** Traditional forms of Witchcraft will argue that the term "Ancestors" applies only to those in your family line that have preceded you. In the Witchcraft of Spectaculus, Ancestors can include anyone who is on the Otherside who has given you a new belief system or core value life inspiration. My definition of an Ancestor is someone whose life, teachings, and work helped shape part of the person you are today. Your Ancestors could include people like Mr. Rogers or Martin Luther King Jr., if they influenced who you are today and a part of their legacy lives on in you.

✦ **THE BONES:** The Bones is the phrase I use for adding your personal artistic essence to your spells, like writing a poem, singing a song, creating a ritual dance, or painting a magickal symbol. See pages 48–49.

- ✦ **CHARGING AN OBJECT:** This is when you transfer your energy, usually through the palms of your hands or through your breath, to put your vision, intention, or power into an object.

- ✦ **CONJURE CASTING:** This term refers to a clear and focused statement of what you want to manifest when casting an effective spell. Phrasing is vital. Be bold. Use confident, focused words like "I am" and "I have." Never use words like "I wish" or "I want" because they're ineffectual; they will keep you wishing and wanting forever.

- ✦ **THE ELECTRIC:** The phrase I use to describe self-love. The Electric is a core belief in your own power, presence, and truth.

- ✦ **A FAMILIAR:** A loyal animal companion of a Witch. The two are deeply tied in spirit, emotion, and magick workings. A Familiar and a Witch walk together, connected by a stronger bond than human language can define. In Bohemia, animals were seen as protectors and teachers because of their otherworldly heightened senses and focused natural instinct. When we allow our Familiar to be a teacher, we gain a greater understanding of instinct and our own Wild magick.

- ✦ **GRIMOIRE:** A magickal book filled with spells, potions, enchantments, and charms.

- ✦ **THE INVITATION:** The phrase I use for the act of calling upon supernatural inspirations of yours to help guide you in your journey. I explain this in further detail on pages 43–47.

- ✦ **THE MUSES:** When I refer to the Muses, I am talking about the unseen goddesses of creativity and art who strike us with inspiration and moments of recognition. In Greek mythology, there were three original muses: Melete, the muse of meditation, contemplation, and thought; Aoide, the muse of voice and song; and Mneme, the muse of memory.

- **THE OTHERSIDE, or the AFTERLIFE:** The Otherside is the realm where we go when we leave this physical world and move to the next plane. My Grandma Helen believed the Otherside is a vibrant and higher plane of being and understanding. She believed that there is no death and we continue on there.

- **THE PENTAGRAM:** The pentagram is a five-pointed star that symbolizes air, fire, water, earth, and spirit. In Spectaculus Witchcraft, the pentagram point is a positive and powerful reminder of our connection to the elements and to our own Wild spirit and the Spirits above.

- **"SEE IT. BE IT. SO BE IT":** The phrase we use in Spectaculus Witchcraft to seal a spell and cast it off into the Universe.

- **SORCERY SIGNATURE:** The phrase I use for adding your hair, saliva, fingernails, or blood to a spell. Because they contain your unique DNA, these items are your magickal signature and they will strengthen your spells. See pages 50–53.

- **SPIRIT HAND:** Your nondominant hand. In Bohemian magick, it is believed that a magickal person has one hand for themselves and the other to work with the Spirits. Because you have less control over your nondominant hand, it is believed that the Spirits have greater ease working through that one.

- **THE SPIRITS:** The Spirits are what I refer to as a combination of loved ones (both people and animals) that have crossed over to the Otherside as well as Ancestors that you have not personally known in this lifetime but who look out for you. My Grandma believed we are assigned Guardians at birth. She also believed that the Spirits take care of us, guide us on our path, and open doors of opportunity or blessings. In my version of praying, the Spirits are who I talk to.

- **THE WILD:** Your truest self. The essence of your being, the version of yourself where ancient magick lies.

ACKNOWLEDGMENTS

I would like to acknowledge with deepest respect the Witches who came before me, the Witches of the present, and the Witches of the future who will keep this work alive. We will ride together forever.

My deepest gratitude to Carolyn Turgeon, who believed in my sorcery enough to introduce me to her editor at HarperCollins and spark this book into existence. To my editor, Elizabeth Viscott Sullivan, thank you for dedicating your artful eye and your deeply creative spirit to this story. I know that Grandma Helen had a supernatural hand in our soulful pairing (Thelma and Louise!). Thank you for burning the midnight oil with me countless times to cast this spell out into the world! I'd also like to thank Raphael Geroni, for creating his own powerful spell with his exquisite book design, and Harper Design Production Director Susan Kosko and Art Director Lynne Yeamans for their work to make this book a treasure.

My love and thanks to Dad, the "Big Dude," for raising me on rock and roll, teaching me to make life a beautiful adventure, and for always believing in this "Little Dude." To Mom, the beautiful Susie Lee, for writing a diary for me before I was born and reading me the stories that made me love books. To my brother, Rion, for being a force of positive magick in this world. To Grandma Irene, Mark, Lulu, and Rusty, for their love and support. To Robert, Marsha, and Lolo Garfinkel for their encouragement about this book during our many beautiful walks together.

I am grateful to my chosen family of performers at the Slipper Room for teaching me the magick of burlesque. To James and Camille Habacker and to James Kenny, who opened the door to all. To Jo Weldon, who took me under her wing and showed me the power of sisterhood. In my Afterlife, I am on the Slipper Room stage with all of you, and every night ends with Uncle Earl (RIP) belting out "Sweet Caroline."

To Burke Heffner: You were with me on most of the journey that I wrote about in this book. You helped change my life with your support and creativity, as you encouraged me to dedicate my life to my magick. Thank you.

To Witch Campers past, present, and future: Thank you for all the unforgettable adventures, many of which have been shared in this book. Our days and nights together are some of the greatest treasures of my life. You each have a place in my heart for always. Remember.

To my Tree, Contessa Hinderliter: Every lifetime we do our magick together, my Sister, is priceless. To Kristi Klein, thank you for enthusiastically reading every version of this book, for believing in me, and for being the badass Witch that you are. Forever Fam. My thanks to the Art Witches, Katelan Foisy, Julia Popescu, Jennifer Dodson, and Ruby Rodriguez, who contributed their magickal work to this book.

My deepest thanks to the Witches and Warlocks who answered my texts at all hours of the night with advice on the book and who did spells to make it happen: Neil Gaiman, David Nielsen, Gina Gershon, Silvana Perelli Vasaka, Sage Sovereign, Nicole Cox, Vanessa Mercedes, and Jaye Bartell.

To Mama Louise, Barbara Biziou, and the magickal world of Sesame Street for being legendary teachers. To the Chelsea Hotel Coven and Tony Notarberardino: Thank you for keeping the portal open and welcoming us all.

To my husband, David Garfinkel Varlow, you cast your spell on me, my life, and this book. You are the divine Magician who seeks out the beauty in the natural world and the sweet adventures in the story of our days. In this book is the magick of our Coney Island nights, the good vibes of our long summer bike rides, the enchantment of New Orleans, and the dark speakeasies where we listened to Sam Cooke and I fell in love with you.

As I finish writing these words, my familiar Niney is curled beside me, and I feel the presence of all my animal friends on the Otherside: Sneaky, Kaiser, Poof, and my dear Greta. The room is filled with the beloved Spirits who guided me to write the last pages of this book: Jeff Moody, Jim Rogers, Grandpa Tom, Grandpa Warren, and of course—always and forever—beautiful Grandma Helen. You are here with me—alive and electric with love. Death is not the end.

PHOTOGRAPHY AND ILLUSTRATION CREDITS

Alamy: 4–5: Heritage Image Partnership Ltd./Alamy Stock Photo; 8: Ian Dagnall Computing/Alamy Stock Photo; 23: Incamerastock/Alamy Stock Photo; 31, jewels in collage: Greg C. Grace/Alamy Stock Photo; 48: Nicola Ferrari/Alamy Stock Photo; 52: The Reading Room/Alamy Stock Photo; 58: Album/Alamy Stock Photo; 59: Classic Image/Alamy Stock Photo; 64: MediaPunch Inc/Alamy Stock Photo; 66–67: Mauritius Images GmbH/Alamy Stock Photo; 68: Historic Collection/Alamy Stock Photo; 72: The Picture Art Collection/Alamy Stock Photo; 98–99: Peter Horree/Alamy Stock Photo; 114: Album/Alamy Stock Photo; 119, top layer: Craig Ellenwood/Alamy Stock Photo; 127: Vintage_Space/Alamy Stock Photo; 155, background: Joerg Metzner/Restless Photography/Stockimo/Alamy Stock Photo; 180, top layer: V&A Images/Alamy Stock Photo; 180, bottom layer: Zoonar GmbH/Alamy Stock Photo; 184, top layer: steeve–x–art/Alamy Stock Photo; 193, bottom layer: MadPhotos/Alamy Stock Photo; 196: Jamal White /Alamy Stock Photo; 209: MkFloral/Alamy Stock Photo; 214: Cultura Creative RF/Alamy Stock Photo, 216: EyeBrowz/Alamy Stock Photo; 218–219: Susan Candelario/Alamy Stock Photo.

Albert, Katrin: 28–29, 33, 34–35, 112–113, 123, 138, 197, 240.

Bridgeman Images: 37: Globe Photos/Zumapress/Bridgeman Images; 50: United Archives GmbH/Bridgeman Images.

Darling, Gala: 183.

Foisy, Katelan: 84–85, 133.

Heffner, Burke: 1, bottom right; 13; 51; 80–81; 83; 88; 91; 92–93; 102; 115; 120–121; 142–143; 155, bottom; 157; 163; 170; 187; 199; 201–203; 220, bottom center; 225; 228; 233.

Llewellyn, Maeve: 2.

Notarberardino, Tony: 49, 55, 57.

Pexels: 1, background: Flora Westbrook; 15: Lisa Fotios; 47: Lukáš Dlutko; 98–99, background: Stacey Gabrielle Koenitz–Rozells; 104–105: Suzy Hazelwood; 119, background, Artem Saranin; 134: Francesco Ungaro; 136–137: Pixabay; 150: Brett Sayles; 158: Pexels Photo Collections; 178: Flora Westbrook; 191: Suzy Hazelwood; 232–233, background: Oleg Magni.

Popescu, Julia (Snakes for Hair): 31, 40, 62, 164, 189, 204.

Rodriguez, Ruby (Poisoned Doll Co.): 87.

Shutterstock: Shutterstock/Valentin Agapov: 49 (frame); Shutterstock/Andrekart Photography: 64 (roses); Shutterstock/Antares Light: 147 (envelope); Shutterstock/Azurel: 89 (key); Shutterstock/Oksana Bernatskaia: 1, 2, 21, 22, 37, 38, 81, 82, 100, 101, 129, 130, 161, 162, 183, 194, 221, 222, 239, 240, (stain); Shutterstock/Katrina Brown: 86 (gold frame); Shutterstock/Denis Burdin: 189 (middle layer of collage; Shutterstock/Mark Carrel: 2 (paper); Shutterstock/Chaikom: 8, 9, 14, 15, 24, 26, 108, 110 (watercolor); Shutterstock/donatas1205: 40, 189, 204 (paper); Shutterstock/DarkBird: 6–7 (frame); Shutterstock/DarkBird: 52, 58–59, 61, 164 (frame); Shutterstock/Valerii Evlakhov: 1–3, 6, 7, 9–59, 61, 62, 64, 65, 68, 69–75, 78–83, 86, 87, 89, 91–97, 100–123, 125–140, 142–151, 153–172, 174, 175, 177–186, 188–211, 213, 214, 216–220, 224, 226–228, 231, 234, 237, 239, 240 (masking tape); Shutterstock/foto.grafs: 125 (matches); Shutterstock/Carolyn Franks: 9, 30, 36, 41, 43, 48, 50, 54, 60, 65, 72, 86, 89, 108, 114, 122, 126, 132, 139, 146, 148, 162, 165, 171, 175, 185, 198, 205, 211, 214, 234, 240 (torn cardboard); Shutterstock/Stephanie Frey: 90, 92, 94, 96 (grunge texture); Shutterstock/Marina Frost 31 (eye of collage; Shutterstock/Happie Hippie Chick: 11, 224 (photo corners); Shutterstock/Here: 4–5, 112–113 (paper); Shutterstock/Inhabitant B: 55, 135, 153 (photo strip frame); Shutterstock/Jizu: 30, 86 (label); Shutterstock/Nerijus Juras: 183 (frame); Shutterstock/jwblinn: 166; Shutterstock/Tara Kompaniets: 31 (frame); Shutterstock/Dimitris K: 216, 224 (frame); Shutterstock/Dmitri Krasovski: 196 (frame); Shutterstock/ Dmitri Krasovski: 199, 203 (frame); Shutterstock/ Tommy Liggett: 226–227;

Shutterstock/LiliGraphie: 11, 12 (vintage paper); Shutterstock/LiliGraphie: 25–26 (frames); Shutterstock/Liligraphie: 39 (photo album); Shutterstock/Liligraphie: 91 (frame); Shutterstock/Liligraphie: 119, 127, 145, 163, 204, 214 (paper); Shutterstock/P Maxwell Photography: 91, 107, 135, 220 (frames); Shutterstock/Media Whalestock: 164 (middle layer of collage; Shutterstock/Mega Pixel: 220 (tickets); Shutterstock/Filip Miletic: 234, 236 (graph paper); Shutterstock/MM photos: 87, 119, 129 (paper); Shutterstock/MM photos: 127 (paper); Shutterstock MM photos: 158 (paper); Shutterstock/nikkytok: 9 (black plastic-tape alphabet); Shutterstock/ninanaina: 164, 189, 204 (watercolor); Shutterstock/Lou Oates: 2, 14, 37, 233 (photo corners); Shutterstock/Lou Oates: 12 (frame); Shutterstock/Lou Oates: 13, 36, 155 (frames); Shutterstock/Lou Oates: 36 (frame); Shutterstock/Lou Oates: 234–236 (frame); Shutterstock/Alekseeva Ohsana: 1, 8, 240 (antique paper); Shutterstock/OooddySmile Studio: 12, 30, 39, 84, 85, 86, (black tape); Shutterstock/Paladin12: 189, 204 (paper); Shutterstock/J.Paly: 31 (underlayer of collage); Shutterstock/paullos: 1 (frame); Shutterstock/pernsanitfoto: 12, 22 (watercolor stains); Shutterstock/PhotoTodos: 12 (frame); Shutterstock/Pongstorn Pix: 47 (lens flare); Shutterstock/Marko Poplasen: 205 (frames); Shutterstock/Theeradech Sanin: 175, 189, 204, 209 (paper); Shutterstock/Shutterstock/schanz: 89, 90, 93–96 (burnt holes); Shutterstock/Jeffrey Schmieg: 55, 153 (photo strip frame); Shutterstock/Alfio Scisetti: 79, 164, 189, 204, 216, 226, 227 (paper); Shutterstock/spatuletail: 146 (stamps); Shutterstock/Studio DMM Photography, Designs & Art: 1, 30, 232 (photo corners); Shutterstock/Studio DMM Photography, Designs & Art: 6, 7, 87, 171, 225, 229, 230, 231, 240 (photo corners); Shutterstock/successo images: 1, 16–18, 31, 32, 53, 54, 57, 58, 94, 114, 117, 185, 186, 220, 237, 238 (paper); Shutterstock/successo images: 1, 20, 65, 68, 71, 72, 75, 76, 108, 240 (paper); Shutterstock/successo images: 13, 37, 38, 43, 44, 46, 49, 50, 81, 82, 87, 100, 103, 127, 128, 131, 132, 159, 160, 164–168, 177, 178, 181, 182, 195, 196, 204, 211, 212, 226, 227 (paper); Shutterstock/successo images: 117, 118, 123, 124, 147, 148, 153–156, 205, 206, 223–225 (paper); Shutterstock/successo images: 139, 140 (paper); Shutterstock/successo images: 171–174, 199, 200, 203, 204, 215, 216 (paper); Shutterstock/Rachata Teyparsit: 228–231 (grunge texture); Shutterstock/Varuna: 100–101 (paper); Shutterstock/Massimo Vernicesole: 146 (envelope); Shutterstock/Peter Versnel: 12, 13, 232 (violets); Shutterstock/Peter Versnel: 12, 13, 233 (violets); Shutterstock/vetre: endpapers, 19 (cyanotype); Shutterstock/Victorian Traditions: 2 (roses); Shutterstock/VicW: 77, 131, 144 (wine stain); Shutterstock/vierra: 102 (frames); Shutterstock/worker: 170 (stained paper); Shutterstock/vovan: 60–61; Shutterstock/xpixel: 1, 3, 19, 31, 60, 61, 89, 91, 97, 98, 99, 107, 115, 119, 125, 145, 155, 157, 163, 196, 209, 216, 217, 225–228, 232–236, 240 (black tape).

Turgeon, Carolyn: 188.

Unsplash: 20–21: Serena Repice Lentini; 68, background: Robert Katzki; 76–77: Gian D. Jzxairpkhho; 135: Annie Spratt; 164, background of collage: J. Lee; 175: Nixx Elle; 176–177: Sophia Ayame; 188: Krystal Ng; 190: Brecht Denil; 194–195: Austin Chan; 220, bottom left: Ankit Dembia; 220, bottom right: Sebastien Cordat.

Varlow, Veronica (author's personal collection): 1, bottom left; 11; 12; 14; 19; 39; 45; 74; 107; 108–109; 122; 129; 140; 144; 151; 153; 166; 171; 193, middle; 205; 210–211; 224; 232.

Front and back covers: flower background: Pexels: blackflowerspexels-irina-iriser-1090972: photograph by Irina Iriser.

Front cover: Shutterstock/bomg: Victorian border; Shutterstock/Katrina Brown; black book cover and small gold frame: Shutterstock/Mark Carrel: distressed paper; Shutterstock/Studio DMM Photography, Designs & Art (photo corners [2]); Shutterstock/Oleg Gekman: eye; Greg C. Grace/Alamy Stock Photo: green gemstones; Shutterstock/Jizu: label; Shutterstock/OooddySmile Studio: black tape 2; Shutterstock/rangizzz: blank picture frame; Shutterstock/xpixel: black tape 1.

BOHEMIAN MAGICK

Copyright © 2021 by VERONICA VARLOW

All rights reserved. No part of this book may be used or reproduced
in any manner whatsoever without written permission except in the
case of brief quotations embodied in critical articles and reviews.
For information address Harper Design, 195 Broadway,
New York, NY 10007.

HarperCollins books may be purchased for educational, business,
or sales promotional use. For information, please e-mail the
Special Markets Department at SPsales@harpercollins.com.

First published in 2021 by
HARPER DESIGN
An Imprint of HarperCollins *Publishers*
195 Broadway
New York, NY 10007
Tel: (212) 207-7000
Fax: (855) 746-6023

harperdesign@harpercollins.com
www.hc.com

Distributed throughout the world by
HarperCollins *Publishers*
195 Broadway
New York, NY 10007

ISBN 978-0-06-302738-1
Library of Congress Control Number: 2020044751

Book design by RAPHAEL GERONI

Printed in Malaysia

First Printing, 2021

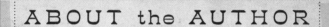

ABOUT the AUTHOR

VERONICA VARLOW IS THE LAST OF A LINE OF BOHEMIAN Witches, a fourth-generation intuitive, and an international burlesque showgirl. She is a confidence and sensuality coach who has been featured on the *Tonight Show*, *Playboy*, CNN, and MTV in 150 countries worldwide. Veronica and her husband, David Garfinkel-Varlow, established the branch of Witchcraft known as Spectaculus, an intersection of the Bohemian magick legacy of Veronica's grandmother Helen and Garfinkel-Varlow's rock-and-roll pagan practices, which stem from natural mysticism and instinctive creativity. Veronica is also one of the cofounders of the infamous Chelsea Hotel Coven in New York City and the founder of Witch Camp, held at the Magick House in Woodstock, New York. Her client list includes Chanel, Tiffany & Co., *Vogue*, Marc Jacobs, Creative Time with David Byrne, and the Whitney Museum of American Art. She performs love rituals, couples' rituals, and healing rituals all over the underground art scene in New York City at events curated by House of Yes, Shanghai Mermaid, Dances of Vice, Lust, Vox Noctem, and You Are So Lucky. She also writes a regular column called "Life of a Love Witch" for *Enchanted Living* magazine. Veronica lives in Brooklyn, crafting spells and making magick with David and her Familiar, the half-wolf half-chihuahua known as Niney. For more adventures, visit www.loveWitch.com and follow her on Instagram @veronicavarlow.